FOOTPRINTS OF
PAUL

FOOTPRINTS OF
PAUL

A modern traveller follows the
trail of Christ's greatest champion

DAVID MARSHALL

AUTUMN

HOUSE

Other books by the same author
Where Jesus Walked (1986)
Breadfruit, Buccaneers and the Bounty Bible (1987)
The Battle for the Book (1991)
The Devil Hides Out (1991)
New Age Versus the Gospel (1993)
Pilgrim Ways (1993)
Is God Still in the Healing Business? (1994)
All published by Autumn House

An Introduction to the Life and Works of John Bunyan (1989)
Published by Bishopsgate

Cover photograph: ACE/Etienne Poupinet
All other photographs: David Marshall

ISBN 1-873796-50-1

Published by
Autumn House
Alma Park, Grantham, Lincolnshire, NG31 9SL, England

FOOTPRINTS OF
PAUL

CONTENTS

About the author:
Dr. David Marshall is one of the most prolific
Christian writers in Britain at the present time. Like
Footprints of Paul his *Where Jesus Walked* (1986)
and *Pilgrim Ways* (1993) are a blend of
contemporary adventure with biblical and historical
insights. The author has a first degree and a PhD
from the University of Hull. His background
includes teaching and preaching, as well as writing
and editing. He is married, lives in Lincolnshire and
is part of a large three-tiered family.

Bible readings are given at the conclusion of each
chapter.
These are for those who • use this book as a basis
for study on the Life, Times and Teachings of Paul;
• use it as a travel guide to the places Paul visited,
and require directions to the appropriate biblical
passages; or • wish to read in full the Bible passages
on which the chapter is based.
Bible quotations in the text are taken from the New
International Version, except where indication is
given to the contrary.

THANKS
to Nan Tucker, Dr. Hugh Dunton and
Dr. John Walton for reading this book in
manuscript form, and for their corrections
and constructive criticisms
to Gloria and Anita for setting the manuscript
and to Anita for her company over the many
years during which I followed the
footprints of Paul.

IN SEARCH OF PAUL

From Christianity's fiercest persecutor, Paul became the Gospel's greatest champion. From the Pharisees' most uncompromising legalist, Paul became the most winsome exponent of God's grace. From a hate-driven crusader, Paul became a love-led, world-travelled promoter of the peace of Christ. And, as anyone who knows nothing else about Paul will tell you — the transformation was sudden, and happened on the Road to Damascus.

Paul was one of the most controversial figures of his own day, as he is of ours. The author of the world's greatest panegyric on love — 'and now abides faith, hope and love, these three . . . ' — is at the crux of the conflict between charismatics and non-charismatics, feminists and anti-feminists, preachers of predestination and defenders of free will, not to mention candleholders for cheap grace, free grace and no grace!

A study of Paul's most comprehensive statement of theology — the Letter to the Romans — has sparked every genuine, lasting revival and reformation in the history of the Christian faith.

Jesus made the atonement. Paul explained it.

The life, death and resurrection of Jesus were the substance of the Gospel. Paul told us how and why.

Paul was the greatest theologian of Scripture and, almost certainly, the most educated of the Bible writers.

All this I knew when I set out on my quest. My quest was for Paul the man. To get to grips with the person of Paul might, I thought, enable me to unravel an enigma I had always believed to be at the core of his thinking.

My quest for Paul, in company with my wife, took me tens of thousands of miles in or on every conceivable mode of transport. Paul's first missionary journey alone involved him in over 1,000 miles of walking; we travelled the same route, but more comfortably. On his second journey he travelled from one end of Anatolia to the other. It is possible to calculate that he travelled 3,500 miles by sea . . . .

Our search for Paul took us to all the great cities where he preached on his love-led journey. In searing September heat we stood on Mars Hill where he preached to the Athenians. In a February freeze-up we went to where the Lystran mob almost beat the life out of him. In a midday heat-shimmer we saw Straight Street, Damascus, and, in our mind's eye, a blinded Jew being led to his lodgings. Early spring sunshine found us in Ephesus, sitting on the outer perimeter of the theatre that once echoed to the cry, 'Great is Artemis of the Ephesians!'

There was the unforgettable, glistening calcified mountainside between Hierapolis and Laodicea. There was the day in Corinth, sun sinking, and, in our mind's eye, Paul preaching to the cosmopolitan crowd — as the 1,000 prostitute priestesses made their nightly journey down from the acropolis to the city. There were sun-warmed days on Cyprus and Malta. There was the Lithostratos where a Jerusalem mob howled for Paul's blood, as they had once howled for the life of his Master. And there was Rome, where, under Nero's tyranny, Paul's life was ended by a sword's blade; and the undying echo, 'For me to live is Christ, to die is gain . . . .'

The importance of the threat posed by Paul may be estimated by the fact that it took 'a detachment of two hundred soldiers, seventy horsemen and two hundred spearmen' (Acts 23:23) to escort him from Jerusalem to Caesarea following his arrest. It speaks volumes for Paul the man that, though under guard by a detachment of the Imperial Regiment, he alone had enough courage to take command of a ship with a complement of 276 in a two-week winter storm.

Paul was far from being a loner. He inspired tremendous loyalty, as well as tremendous opposition. His travels from place to place enabled him to establish a network of friends and believers across most of the Roman Empire. His letters to them are part of the New Testament and, aside from their theological and biographical content, we learn much of the men and women on Paul's 'team'. He mentions them by name, never neglecting to detail their individual contributions to the cause of the Gospel.

The works of the Roman historians of the period, particularly those of Gaius Suetonius and Cornelius Tacitus, add both colour and exlanation to events happening in an Empire over which Tiberius, Caligula, Claudius and Nero presided.

Our travels from Tarsus, where Paul was born, to Rome where his life ended, took us through the Middle East, Turkey, Greece, Italy and the islands of the Mediterranean. On some of our travels we were a party of two. On others we joined groups organized by Christian tour companies like Peltours, Highway and Inter-Church.

Our hope is that when you have read the story of our adventures you will want to follow the footprints of Paul yourself; but, more importantly, you will come to know Paul the man and, thus, unravel that enigma that can get in the way when we read his writings.

Most importantly, we hope that our trek in the footprints of Paul and our insights into the church groups to whom Paul wrote his great letters, will enable you to gain a clearer understanding of the good news this apostle to the Gentiles gave his life to proclaim.

Our journey begins at an airport near you. If you have your passport and boarding card, you are ready to begin with us a journey to the world of the apostles . . . .

DAVID MARSHALL

1 ROME: CENTRE OF THE WORLD

The plane began to slant slowly earthwards, into a violet evening. And there was Rome, embalmed, as ever, in the past but throbbing with the pulse of the present.

Rome, we had decided, was the necessary port of entry to the world of the apostles. From the banks of the Tiber men had gone out to conquer an empire, had networked that empire with roads, had imposed upon it Hellenistic culture and had continued the struggle to hold down the troublesome tribes by the force of disciplined legions.

Our quest would have to begin there: the centre of the world.

As we circled in to land, the sea glittered in the mauve-lemon light of the fading afternoon. It seemed a long time since our early-morning start; cold and grey with the hint of rain, a standard design for March mornings in our part of England.

Once we had cleared the white cliffs, the flight out had been surprisingly idyllic. We had caught a clear view of the Somme estuary as we had flown into France, followed by a wonderful view of Lake Geneva — and, beyond it, the snow-covered high alps rising like the Kingdom of the Ice Queen. There had been the savage splendour of the snow-flanked, ice-veined, jagged peaks. At one point, as a wing dipped, we had seemed surrounded from horizon to horizon by alpine peaks; it had looked like the surface of another planet.

But on the foothills there was no more than a dusting of snow. Spread out beyond: the grey sprawl of industrial northern Italy.

Then, as we circled in to land at Rome airport, the nearby sea-coast lay drowsing in the violet of approaching nightfall. The coast was a great deal closer than Rome itself, which we had seemed to leave behind by more than the usual margin of miles between a capital and its airport.

Baggage collected, as per travel agent's instruction, we

looked out for someone with the travel company's placard to bus us to our hotel in Rome. The English-speaking passengers disappeared from the terminal as if by magic. We were left surrounded by loud, gesticulating Italians greeting stout relations off other flights.

After an hour — and no travel company placard — one solitary Englishman hove to, with his daughter Sarah. He had, it turned out, flown in on the same flight and searched the air terminal in vain for the vital placard. He was philosophical. At his suggestion we went in search of a railway station. In Italy, we discovered, train tickets were to be bought in newspaper kiosks. The vendor, to give him his due, tried to explain something to us. But he spoke in rapid Italian . . . .

In no time, luggage, wife and self were shoved into the empty spaces in a crowded late-night commuter train. My perch was next to a large, red-faced man. As soon as he began to speak I identified his accent as belonging to the tiny patch of northern England that was once my home. Now, it appeared, he was head of Scotrail and had come to learn what he could from Italian railways.

None of this was of any help when the commuter train decanted us at the Stazione Ostiense terminus. A swift glance at the map confirmed that this was the opposite side of Rome from our hotel in the Via Cavour. Nonetheless, this blunder had its plus side. We were in Rome to follow the footsteps of the apostles. And we were warm already! Across the road from the Ostiense terminus was the Porta San Paolo. And, as we would discover in the light of day, we were a short walk away from the site of Paul's tomb over which Constantine had built the Basilica of San Paolo. Constantine's basilica was gutted by fire in 1823 and was subsequently replaced by the vast Church of St. Paul that one visits today.

But Paul was not uppermost in my thinking as I haggled with the taxi driver. As he hurtled us through the ancient city, past a flood-lit Colosseum and a host of other ancient, imposing buildings dating from the days of the caesars, my pulse was racing. The taxi driver was counting on this. As he heaved us and our luggage onto the pavement on the wrong side of the Via Cavour for the Hotel Atlantico, he stung me in Italian currency for the equivalent of a quarter of the Gatwick to Rome air fare!

Lesson one. Avoid Rome taxis if you value your solvency. If you have to use one, negotiate your fare with the driver before the journey begins — *and hold him to it.* The volume of traffic, maniac driving style and impossibility of parking put car hire out of the question. The way to get around in Rome is on foot. When you get really tired, take a tram. But, as you stand holding on to the rail, watch out for pickpockets . . . .

The noise level in late-night Rome was horrendous. We still had the full benefit of the street roar and honking when we reached our room at the front of the hotel. Using what little Italian she had learned, my wife negotiated for, and secured for us, a much quieter room at the back of the hotel.

In other ancient cities — Jerusalem, Istanbul, Athens — we had always woken in a dither of excited anticipation. Rome had yet to win our confidence. At 7 am, from our quiet room, it was difficult to determine whether the sun shone — or if indeed there was any weather at all! The huge window was so burglar-proof that it was almost air-proof. At length I hoisted the solid blind, opened the window itself, and craned my neck outwards. In March you take your chances with the weather in Rome. But even at that time of morning, bright sunshine shafted the narrow alley from the Via Cavour.

After a continental breakfast of crusty rolls in a huge dining room, we were off. We had studied our map of Rome carefully. Soon we were treading the pavements of the Via Nazionale towards the sites of antiquity. In every direction were imposing buildings. It looked as if Michelangelo's successors had maintained an evocative standard of architecture in most parts of the city. Even where it is decayed and crumbling it has character, atmosphere and an air of Renaissance.

With the Trajan Column we began to discover the historical period that the Renaissance revived. For a nominal fee we entered ancient Rome. And, in so doing, stepped into a vast, archaeological site covering the Capitol and Palatine Hills and the valleys between. We were back in the age of the caesars; the men whose names and actions provided the political backdrop to the New Testament. On Palatine Hill were the excavations of the palaces of the first few caesars; Augustus, Tiberius, Caligula, Claudius, Nero. They had built their palaces on that hill, each one building to outdo his predecessor.

Below was the Roman Forum and the Forum of Augustus. Off the Via Sacra were the impressive remains of the Basilica Aemilia and the Temple of Antonius and Faustina. At the end of the Via Sacra was the arch that celebrated the victories of Septimius Severus. From it, in the opposite direction, could be seen the Arch of Titus: built to commemorate his victories in the Judaic campaign of AD70 that involved the destruction of Jerusalem. And then, by the side of the Colosseum, the largest of the arches in Rome: the Arch of Constantine.

Within half a mile, an impressive artefact to Augustus, the Caesar whose census made necessary a journey from Nazareth to Bethlehem and who, in the very year of the Bethlehem birth, announced his own godhead . . . excavations of the palaces and commemorations of the deeds of the very caesars who persecuted Christianity in its infancy: Nero, Domitian and Trajan . . . and the great arch of the Emperor who did Christianity a doubtful favour by declaring it the official religion of the Roman Empire . . . .

We spent some thoughtful hours in the Colosseum, the greatest of all monuments to the persecution of early Christianity.

The imperial reign of Augustus (27BC–AD14) was a great age for construction. However, his proud boast, 'I found Rome built of brick; I leave it clothed in marble,' was just that. His massive forum, his Temple of Mars and his Theatre of Marcellus were impressive, but hardly changed the aspect of a city big enough to accommodate 750,000 souls (in six square miles). The building (intact) that fired my imagination was one Augustus coaxed his son-in-law and counsellor, Marcus Agrippa, to build in the year of his accession: the splendidly-columned rotunda topped with a dome and known as the Pantheon. Fronting a typical Roman square, cluttered with chairs and canopied tables, with the inevitable fountain, this was a perfect place for afternoon reflection . . . .

Those eight grey granite columns shaded that same colossal door when Rome martyred Peter in AD67, when Paul entered the city by the Appian Way in AD61, when a Galilean Jew called Jesus was crucified outside Jerusalem in AD31 in the reign of Augustus's successor, Tiberius, when the thin cry of a man-child pierced the midnight clear at Bethlehem at the crossroads of time . . .

That cry and crucifixion, the Gospel that Paul brought and that Peter was put to death for preaching were, in ages to come, to echo around the world. But there, at the world's centre, those events went largely unnoticed when they happened. For Rome had more important concerns . . . .

Readings
>   Luke 2:1-20
>   John 18:28-19:16

2 NO MEAN CITY

At the time of the obscure birth on a remote frontier that would become the focus of the centuries, Augustus's Empire encompassed around eight million people and stretched from the Channel coast to the Syrian desert.

Augustus had brought peace. The conflicts that had fractured Rome in the days of the Republic had ended. When, at the Battle of Philippi, Marc Antony had settled all scores arising from the assassination of Julius Caesar, 19-year-old Octavian (Augustus), an unlikely candidate for world ruler, had begun to emerge. Marcus Agrippa's defeat of Antony and Cleopatra at Actium in 31BC had ensured that Augustus would accede. After he had entered Rome in triumph, the Senate had conferred upon Augustus all the most powerful positions, including permanent command of the armed forces and *Pontifex Maximus*, chief priest of the ancient civic religion.

Only Judaea, restless since the death of Herod the Great, seemed to threaten the *Pax Romana*. When it rose in rebellion against Herod's son and successor Archelaus, Publius Quintilius Varus, Caesar's governor in Syria, sent the legions, quashed all resistance, and crucified 2,000 insurgents. Their crosses lined the main east-west road that passed beneath the cliff on which Nazareth stood, and made a grisly spectacle for the town's youth who would, at that time, have included Jesus, 'the carpenter's Son'.

The crushing of the rebellion had resulted in the destruction of Sepphoris, the Galilean capital where the rebellion had begun. It was not rebuilt. Client-king Herod Antipas chose to build a new capital by the shores of Lake Galilee. In deference to the new Caesar upon whom the mantle of Augustus had fallen in AD14, he named it Tiberias.

Gaius Suetonius, who wrote his history, *The Twelve Caesars*, when director of the imperial libraries under Trajan (AD98–117), remembered Augustus as the first Emperor to build his palace on Palatine Hill and as a man tolerant of the religious diversity within his Empire. In a letter to Tiberius, Augustus had expressed interest in Jewish faithfulness with regard to their Sabbath observance. In a letter to his grandson Gaius (Caligula), however, Augustus applauded his refusal to offer prayers in Jerusalem. There were limits, apparently.

The nuisance potential of the Jews was multiplied by the fact that Jewish communities were to be found in most cities of the Eastern Empire. Among these cities — 'no mean city' according to its celebrated son — was Tarsus. And while Jesus had opportunity to witness the awful brutality of Rome from the hill at Nazareth, the celebrated son of Tarsus was enjoying an altogether more privileged position under the Empire.

In the ancient Jewish community of Tarsus, Paul would have been known by his Hebrew name, Saul. He was born three or four years after the Bethlehem birth. He would have been raised on stories of a fabulous event which had taken place at Tarsus thirty years earlier, and that would never be erased from the folk memory of the proud city.

Following his victory at Philippi, Antony had chosen to rest in Tarsus. From there he summoned the beautiful Queen Cleopatra of Egypt to appear before him and receive her ritual humiliation for the support she had given to his enemies. Cleopatra had decided to outshine the Roman general by something more than the usual royal pageantry. While Antony waited on his throne in the marble streets of Tarsus, the Egyptian fleet had appeared, approaching the city through the Lake of Rhegma. The crowd had seen it and vanished from the immediate vicinity of Antony who, in consequence, sat in splendid isolation. Cleopatra's purple-sailed, gold-sterned vessel, its silver oars moving in time to an orchestra, approached in fabulous fashion. Perfumes wafted ashore as Cleopatra herself appeared to Antony's astonished gaze — dressed as Aphrodite, goddess of Love.

'I am a Jew of Tarsus . . . ,' wrote Paul, 'of the people of Israel, of the tribe of Benjamin, a Hebrew of the Hebrews; in regard to the Law, a Pharisee; as for zeal, persecuting the church; as for legalistic righteousness, faultless.' And all that was true. Paul's father was a burgess of the city. Since, by a reform fifteen years before Paul's birth, the rank of citizen had been withdrawn from all those except wealthy property owners, it may be inferred that he was a *rich* burgess. The title *civis Romanus* (Citizen of Rome) was a sought-after one given either by way of reward for services rendered or in return for a fat fee. Both Paul and his father carried that distinction; it was hereditary. Wherever they might travel within the Roman world, Roman citizenship should have ensured certain specific rights and privileges.

Whatever wealth Paul's father had accumulated would have been through his skill as a tent maker and a trader. The master tent maker of Tarsus would have worked both in leather and in *cilicium*, cloth woven from the long hair of the black goats that grazed then, as now, on the foothills of the Taurus Mountains behind Tarsus. *Cilicium* came from the name of the lush plain, Cilicia, between the mountains and the sea. Tarsus was not actually on the coast but, as Cleopatra had found, was easily accessible from the sea by lake and river. The harbour that had witnessed her perfumed arrival was, more usually, a busy trade centre.

Tarsus was a cosmopolitan city. While Paul would have learned his tent-making trade in the Jewish quarter, his business would have brought him into contact with Greeks, Macedons, Persians and Syrians, as well as Jews and indigenous Cilicians. Pagan temples as well as Jewish synagogues abounded in Tarsus. The cultures and religions of many nations converged there. Though 'a Hebrew of the Hebrews', Paul was partly a product of Hellenistic culture, a child of the Roman world, and would have been brought up in constant contact with Gentiles.

While all that inevitably influenced Paul's education and life view, it was not the most powerful influence on his formative years. Like his parents, he was a member of the rigid Jewish sect, the Pharisees. While the term 'pharisee' is synonymous with 'hypocrite' wherever it is known today, Paul's family would have viewed the Pharisees as the Party of Reform. Their aim: strict obedience to the Law of Moses and the endless tangle of mind-warping rules that had accumulated around it. While Paul would have learned Greek and some Latin in early childhood, Aramaic (derived from

Hebrew) would have been spoken at home. The Hebrew text of the Torah to be found at the Tarsus synagogue was everything; all else was secondary, though it was accepted that a working knowledge of the Greek philosophers and poets was more or less indispensable.

While learning to read and write the Scriptures in Hebrew, Paul was also familiar with the sacred writings in their Greek Septuagint form. By exposure to the Scriptures on the Sabbath, at home, and in the School of the Rabbis, Paul would have committed vast tracts of them to memory by the time he was 13. It was in that year Paul moved into higher education. Tarsus had a world-famous university whose teachers included Athenodorus and Nestor. Without neglecting his studies of the Torah, Paul would have studied there.

But the real milestone in Paul's higher education was when he set sail from Tarsus for Joppa and, from thence, went up mountain to Jerusalem. There he 'sat at the feet of Gamaliel'. Gamaliel was a distinguished rabbi and the grandson of Hillel. Paul remained under his tutelage for six years. It is clear that he distinguished himself for both learning and zeal. He was marked out as a future member of the Sanhedrin, the seventy-one men who were, under Rome, the judges and spiritual leaders of occupied Palestine.

While studying under Gamaliel, it has been argued, Paul might have been exposed to the teaching of Jesus and might, indeed, have been a witness to His crucifixion. Given the absence of such details from the many autobiographical passages in his letters and recorded sermons, this would seem improbable. Most likely, after his six years with Gamaliel, Paul returned to the steamy, malarial city on the Cilician Plain, thus being absent from Jerusalem during the crucifixion year. Back in Tarsus he would have made his living as a tent maker and found his fulfilment as an ever-more-distinguished rabbi. Paul's return to Jerusalem and his accession to a seat on the Sanhedrin almost certainly occurred after his thirtieth birthday.

After some years' absence from Tarsus, it would seem that

Paul returned there again, following his Damascus Road conversion and period of retreat in Arabia. Back in the Jewish quarter of the city it is likely that he experienced significant tensions with his family, community and the elders of the synagogue. In AD56 he was to write that on five occasions the Jews punished him with 'forty stripes save one'. None of those whippings is recorded in Acts. Hence it might well have been that some of them were received during the hidden years in Tarsus. There is a tradition that Paul was cast off by home and kindred — and, perhaps, wife — and that he spent some months alone in a cave in the wild country of the Taurus foothills. Modern pilgrims are conducted to 'St. Paul's Cave'. That might, indeed, have been the place where Paul was found when, as a result of the rapid growth of Christianity in Antioch, Barnabas went in search of him as a potential helper. At all events, it was in or near Tarsus that Barnabas recruited Paul in AD41.

When William Ramsay visited Tarsus a century ago, he wrote of 'a city with its feet resting on a great inland harbour and its head reaching up to the hills'. When H. V. Morton came thirty years later, he waxed lyrical about dusty caravans bisecting the Cilician Plain towards the mountain pass, the long-haired goats grazing the lower slopes of the Taurus, the back-street weavers who still made cloth from the goats' long hair (methods and machines almost unchanged from Paul's tent-making days), and the passage of migrating storks overhead.

In the February days when we went in search of Saul of Tarsus, US bombers, not storks, flew from beyond the snow-covered Taurus Mountains over the Cilician Plain — making for Iraq. Whether weavers were working in back streets we could not say. But, as the snow fell with light persistence, melting as it touched the tumbled roofs of the now-Turkish town, our imaginations did glimpse a picture of ancient ships thronging an ancient harbour — and a keen-eyed Jewish youth looking on. There was a place where a lad could have his horizons pushed back, and could develop an itch to travel . . . .

. . . Before him, a procession of ships lifting their sails to pass from that inland port to all points west . . .

. . . Behind him, the great Cilician Gates gashed through the mountain chain; an unbelievable gorge, a haunted pass through which Cyrus and Alexander, in their respective centuries, had marched their armies on mighty campaigns of conquest, and the hordes of Crusaders would one day descend on Tarsus to find a great Byzantine church dedicated to St. Paul.

In Paul's day, of course, the Cilician Gates witnessed only the passage of the legions and of endless camel-trains with destinations like Ephesus, Philippi, Thessalonica and the cities of Galatia . . . .

Readings
  Philippians 3:1-11.
  Acts 9:11; 11:25, 26.
  Acts 21:30-39.

3 DAWN IN JERUSALEM

There is little to compare with the experience of arriving at a small airport in a strange country, hours late — and in the middle of the night. A sleep-befuddled brain, stroked by the heat-felted darkness, was trying to work out a way of fixing a lift across the forty miles of wilderness and mountain between Ben Gurion airport and Jerusalem. I had saved a small fortune by buying a bucket-shop ticket and filling a seat on a charter flight, and the flight had always been scheduled to touch down around midnight. But who could have foreseen the two-hour delay at Heathrow?

Outside the airport, the scents and sounds of the Middle Eastern night whirring my brain back to the adventures of earlier visits, it was clear that things were quieter than usual. Only taxi touts were there in any number; but, as with Rome, it is neither good for your pocket nor their souls that they should be allowed to perpetrate extortion. After a short walk, I found what I was looking for: a stretch limo known as a *sherut*. In Israel, *sheruts* are shared taxis with moderate, fixed fares.

Soon, with baggage strapped on the roof, and a dozen sleepy Slavs for company, I was hurtling through the darkness towards Jerusalem.

Tarsus was the launch-pad for Paul's life and ministry. But Jerusalem was where the events that launched the Christian faith occurred and from whence a jack-booted Sanhedrin member, 'breathing fire and slaughter', had set off on the road to Damascus . . . .

I had never seen the streets of West Jerusalem so empty. The Slavs were dropped off at a modern hotel. I was alone in the back seat of the stretch-limo as we passed the floodlit, west-facing walls of the Old City and the Jaffa Gate. How could I possibly make myself heard at St. Andrews at 4.30am? I recalled, with some nervousness, the evening five years earlier when I had inadvertently set off the security alarm by climbing on to a flat roof to take those Jerusalem-at-night pictures. The Warden, Dr. William Craig, later to be Moderator of the Church of Scotland, had seemed in two minds whether to hand me over to the Israeli police anti-terrorist branch. What would they do to me for waking everyone in that very much wired-for-sound building at 4.30am?

Surrounded by baggage, I timidly knocked on the massive door. In seconds, it was opened by a petite lady, in a heavy-duty dressing-gown — and a smile that brought me fully awake.

'Dr. Marshall, I'd almost given you up for lost. I'm so pleased to see you. My name is Carole Dixon.'

In my three-week stay we were to become firm friends. I was to discover that Carole had an unlisted gift of the Spirit that all believers should covet: *the gift of joy.*

In no time I was alone in my old room in the tower, overlooking the Old City and the Mount of Olives. In the sky above the Mount of Olives, in which a company of angels had once received the ascending Lord out of the sight of men, something was happening. The breath of dawn was replacing the slumber of dark. The blue-grey night sky became engorged with crimson. A fiery orb burst up over the horizon, spurting streams of molten sunlight. The hills and valleys appeared, green and swathed in drifting veils of mist. Dew glittered red in the rising sun. There were more wonders, but I slept through them . . . .

At 9am I interviewed Teddy Kollek, long-time Mayor of Jerusalem. At 11.30 I met Dr. Daniel Rossing, Minister of Religious Affairs in the Likud Government. At noon I attended a lecture by Professor Stephen Kaplan at the Hebrew University. All displayed the same indulgent humour. 'We both believe in the Messiah,' said Rossing. 'But when He comes *we* shall just have to ask Him: Is this your first trip to Israel?'

It was only after a full week of such engagements, punctuated by trips to archaeological sites in company with Harvard-trained archaeologist Dr. William Shea, that I was joined by my wife. At last there was time to consider the great Christ-event of AD31 that made the substance of Paul's Gospel.

The crammed bazaars of the Christian and Muslim quarters of the Old City, crackling with life and roaring with barter, are common to all Arab lands and have little to teach us about the first century. But, wedged in the Eastern corner is the great raised platform where the Dome of the Rock now stands, the Jewish temple once stood. Among its complex of buildings was the Hall of Hewn Stone in which the Sanhedrin met. There Jesus was condemned and, later, Paul was commissioned to extend his persecution of the followers of the risen Christ to Damascus.

The high profile of Islam, the *muezzin* turned to full volume in keeping with the modern resurgence of Muslim fundamentalism, the constant importunities of touts selling anything from olive wood statuettes to guided tours of the city and the cynical exploitation of the credulity of visiting pilgrims by almost everybody, ruins the Jerusalem experience for many visitors. Disappointment can be avoided if we remember three things:
• Jerusalem is sacred to *three* religions, all of which have a right to be represented there. • Touts respond to humour and firm negatives. • Most printed guides to Jerusalem will enable us to extrapolate legend from fact.

In Jerusalem, as with any other New Testament city, familiarize yourself with the biblical significance of each site before you visit and, if possible, read the appropriate New Testament passage *in situ*.

It also helps, of course, to know where to look . . . .

Despite the best efforts of shrine-builders over twenty centuries, the Mount of Olives still offers scope for evocative reflection; walk its steep roadways and visit Gethsemane and the Church of the Agony.

Walk around the walls of the Old City, pausing by St. Stephen's Gate to reflect on what happened close by, three years after the crucifixion . . . .

Paul, now back in Jerusalem; influential in the Sanhedrin . . . the Pharisee party harnessing the zeal of the young rabbi against the followers of Christ . . . the unruly crowd surrounding Stephen; Paul obliged to listen as Stephen expounds the Gospel of Christ crucified and risen . . . Paul's reaction against the tolerant teaching of Gamaliel; his derision of Jesus; his vindictive sarcasm against Stephen . . . the mad rush that ends in a smashed corpse and a pool of blood below the Rock of Execution — the men of violence throwing their clothes symbolically 'at the feet of a young man named Saul . . . '

. . . the beginnings of self-doubt as he recalls to memory the death cry of Stephen: 'Lord Jesus, receive my spirit . . . . Do not hold this sin against them' . . . rising annoyance with himself as he totally fails to banish this memory from his mind and the mounting hatred in his heart as, with greater fierceness, he persecutes the followers of this Christ: makes it his great cause . . . .

It is likely that no site in Jerusalem is more evocative of the Christ-event of AD31 — and the martyrdom of Stephen in AD34 — than a garden two hundred yards north of the Damascus Gate. At one end of this enclosed and quiet place is a skull-shaped hill, below which the ancient Damascus Road ran and which, historically, is associated with executions. At the other end of the peaceful garden is the Garden Tomb: a first-century tomb, outside of which is a groove where a stone would have been rolled into position. In all our visits we have spent many hours in that peaceful place, reflecting on the events of that great Passover weekend. Always we have been in the company of the Revd Bill and Mrs. Gladys White. Associated for half a century with the Garden Tomb, for years — until his retirement in 1990 — Bill White was privileged, each Sunday, to preach a sermon — with the empty tomb, the greatest visual aid of the Christ-event, behind him . . . .

As we sit reverently in this sacred place, it is not difficult to imagine, in the first light of that Sunday morning, Mary of Magdala, bearing the impedimenta of embalming, and concerning herself with the question of who would move the massive stone that blocked the entrance to the tomb. We imagine the devastation when she discovered the stone rolled away, but the tomb empty. Then the unspeakable ecstasy, beyond words to describe, when a familiar voice said, 'Mary'.

We think of those days after the resurrection when, having faced down their initial scepticism, the Risen Christ walked and talked and ate with His disciples. How He commissioned them to wait in Jerusalem for the power of the Spirit to descend upon them. How they saw Him ascend, their ears ringing with His promise, 'I am with you alway, even unto the end of the world.'

Then the days of prayerful, in-one-accord waiting and preparation.

The descent of the Spirit in tongues of fire, while an earthquake shook Jerusalem and a mighty wind rushed through the city's streets.

The surge of the crowd — Jerusalemites and visitors —

towards the temple precincts. Peter's great sermon asserting the death and resurrection of the Messiah. All well within a quarter of a mile of an empty tomb that bore a silent witness to the truth of his striking assertion; an assertion, so easy to disprove had it been untrue.

The heady, early days of the Church: thousands converted, including 'some of the priests' . . . .

The beginning of persecution. Miraculous deliverances. Humble men, who had fled from Gethsemane, been conspicuous by their absence from Calvary, standing heads erect in the Hall of Hewn Stone and fearlessly proclaiming their Gospel to the Sanhedrin.

The increase in the intensity of persecution as the Jewish establishment saw their power, influence and wealth slipping away.

A young rabbi from Tarsus increasingly taking the initiative in the persecution, so that, at the stoning of Stephen, his leadership of the anti-Christian cause was implicitly accepted as the killers cast their clothing at his feet.

The years AD31-34 saw striking, even earth-shaking events in and around Jerusalem. But the earth was not shaken — yet.

While the Son of God gave His life for the sins of mankind and rose a conqueror over sin and death and suffering; and while ordinary men, with extraordinary power, spread the good news of the implications of the Christ-event for mankind to Judaea, Samaria and Syria, in Rome — the centre of the world — there was total unawareness. Indeed, rarely in the memory of anyone then living could a more corrupt regime be recalled. Cornelius Tacitus, in *The Annals of Imperial Rome*, written when he was Senator in the black years of Domitian's imperial reign (AD81-96), told the story . . . .

By AD31 the Emperor Tiberius had withdrawn from Rome to the island of Capri where he spent his time 'in secret orgies, or wild, malevolent thoughts'. Rome, meanwhile, was in the grip of a Reign of Terror organized by Aelius Sejanus. To maintain absolute power, Sejanus played on the superstitions of the reclusive Emperor. No family, however high born, was safe from the lust or malice of Sejanus. There were rumours in Asia and Achaia that members of the imperial family had been murdered at the orders of Sejanus to prepare the way for his own accession to the imperial throne. It is undoubtedly the case that Sejanus proposed marriage to Julia Livilla, sister of the future Emperor Claudius, with that aim in view.

The principal preoccupation in Rome in the year Christ died was 'How can we remove Sejanus?' At one stage Tiberius sailed into the Tiber but dared not land. At length he engineered the downfall of Sejanus by enlisting the co-operation of his deputy, Macro, an even greater brute.

While in AD31-34 the talk in Jerusalem was of a crucifixion, a resurrection, and the massive growth of a new religious movement, the talk in Rome was of a great blood-letting: the revenge of Tiberius and Macro upon the family, friends and followers of Sejanus — numbered in many thousands.

With rumours of the Roman terror flying thick as bats on a summer evening, the slaughter that Paul planned to undertake in the name of God on the Damascus Christians probably seemed of minimal significance.

Hardly had he begun to set his face north, than his anger fired up like a furnace.

He had just passed the site of Stephen's murder.

Readings
>   Acts 1:8-14.
>   Acts 2:1-18, 36-41.
>   Acts 6:8-15.
>   Acts 7:54-8:3.

4 THE ROAD TO DAMASCUS

Figures were approaching, riding through the haze of shimmering silence.

One man out front in isolation, some yards behind him a posse of soldiers. No noise of hooves as they rode full tilt for Damascus. Silence and the noon-heat shimmer.

Then noise. Not from the men nor their animals. An unnatural noise from the skies; more like a voice than thunder. The out-front rider fell. From his position on the ground he seemed to be addressing the Source of the noise. After some hesitation, the other riders, puzzled, reined in around the figure on the ground. They lifted him up. Someone took charge of his mount. Two men dismounted, held him by the arms and led him the remaining distance into the city.

Saul of Tarsus had become a Christian.

The most hard-headed, fanatical exponent of the Final Solution to the Christian Problem — had become a Christian.

The most detailed narrative of his conversion comes from the pen of his biographer, a medical doctor (Acts 9). He provided two other accounts himself. Both became a matter of public record. One was given to the Sanhedrin in the Hall of Hewn Stone (Acts 22:1-21). The other was given to Herod Agrippa at Caesarea (Acts 26:9-23).

The world is still reeling from the repercussions of that conversion.

In Paul's day the Roman Empire had removed all frontiers. Hence Paul and the shock troops of the Sanhedrin — from which, as a Pharisee, he had to keep his distance — could ride direct from Jerusalem to Damascus on the trade route from Egypt to Syria and beyond.

In *our* day we can follow Paul only as far as the Israeli-Syrian border in the Golan. We peer across the high, sun-baked plain towards Damascus from an area rutted with so many tank tracks, it could have been the site of an Armageddon. To complete the journey to Damascus we have to return to London and take another flight, another year. We are even advised to acquire another passport.

'Meanwhile, Saul was still breathing out murderous threats against the Lord's disciples. He went to the high priest and asked him for letters to the synagogues in Damascus, so that if he found any there who belonged to the Way, whether men or women, he might take them as prisoners to Jerusalem . . . .'

It was not that Saul or the Sanhedrin had any jurisdiction in Damascus. Though its religious discipline extended to every Jewish community, it was a measure of both its arrogance and its estimate of the threat posed by Christianity, that the Sanhedrin was prepared to risk reprisals from both the Romans and their client-ruler — the Nabatean King in his red-rock capital, Petra — by authorizing Saul to take life and to take prisoners.

It would be a lonely journey for that Pharisee of the Pharisees. For company he had only his thoughts on that 170-mile journey which, because of the terrain, would have taken about a week. On the Sistene ceiling, Michelangelo has Saul astride a good horse. Since no one in the East walks when he can ride, we can assume that Saul and the Temple Guard would have been astride some mount — horse, camel or donkey.

A lonely journey, with only his thoughts for company. What were they likely to have been?

We thought of this as we followed his route . . . .

The nature of his mission presupposed a mind full of anti-Christian venom; later he said a 'raging fury' had obsessed him (Acts 26:11, RSV). But, aside from his role as Grand Inquisitor, Paul was by nature an intellectual theologian. On a need-to-know basis, Paul needed to know everything there was to know about the beliefs of the opposition. Hence, while Paul had never been exposed directly to Jesus, we can assume that during the years in which he had persecuted the Jerusalem Christians, the young rabbi, from his seat on the Sanhedrin, would have heard leading Christians defend their faith. Through his enquiries he would have made it his business to find out as much as he could about the crucified Nazarene, if only to find information to discredit Him; His life, His teachings, the curious events that had culminated in His execution, and the still more curious events which had transformed a timid group of disciples into bold spokesmen for God in the prophetic mode.

As he set out on the road to Damascus, well within sight of the walls of Jerusalem, he passed the Hill of Execution on the right. His anger boiled; but his rational mind, trained by the best logicians at the University of Tarsus, knew that no bad man could have died as Stephen had died. Paul could still see the light of eternity shining from the eyes of the first Christian martyr.

Soon Paul's party would have been pounding the surface of the steep roads through the lion-coloured hills of Samaria. At every turn there were reminders of the teachings and miracles of the Man who had claimed to be Messiah. As the party, with Paul out front, rode into the broadlands of Galilee — the Valley of Jezreel — the memories of the Nazarene would have been impossible to shrug off. The road passed Cana, Nain — and beneath the rocky cliff on which Nazareth stood.

Galloping by then, Paul's troop on that springtime journey would sight Mount Hermon in the far distance, with its snows that fed the Jordan. But first the road passed through the gash in the Galilean hills called the Horns of Hittin, and so to Magdala. Magdala was a famous nightstopover place for those who journeyed along the Great Road. Paul would have known that a female citizen of that town, having turned from prostitution to the Christian Way, had been the first witness of the resurrection. There were echoes, there, of His teaching: 'No one who comes to me, is ever turned away . . . .' One day he would carry on the echo; 'All manner of sin and blasphemy shall be forgiven unto men . . . .'

After Magdala, the Great Road followed the shoreline of

the Sea of Galilee through Capernaum and Bethsaida. If
Paul had wanted to banish the Nazarene from his mind, had
that banishment been possible, he would have heard the
citizens of those populous towns speaking in great excitement
of the One who had lived among them, healing their sick,
raising their dead . . . .

It is likely that the Capernaum synagogue was still
administered by Jairus who could not forget what the Master
had done for his daughter . . . .

Those were the towns where the Twelve had been
recruited . . . .

The very lake itself was redolent with memories of the
Christ. As he would tell the Corinthians before too many
years had passed, there were 500 men still living who had
seen the Risen Christ; and most of them would have seen
·Him on the Galilean hill on which He had called His
followers together. In Capernaum and Bethsaida, Paul would
have interviewed such witnesses; and, having done so, and
against all his instincts, would have begun to look at the resurrection event as a fact. Might even have begun to puzzle
over the Messianic passages of Scripture in search of evidence
that Messiah had to die . . . . The Lamb without blemish;
slain for the sins of the people . . . an atonement of blood;
justification through the death of the perfect One . . .
remission of sins, through the shedding of blood . . . 'For
Christ's love compels us, because we are convinced that One
died for all, and therefore all died . . . ' . . . the Way of
reconciliation with God: 'God made Him who had no sin to
be sin for us, so that in Him we might become the righteousness of God . . . .'

As the mounts of Paul and the Temple Guard struggled
up the steep slopes of Mount Hermon, Galilee lost below in
the heat mist, Paul was living through the last days of his
unbelief. His internal struggle must have been tremendous.
His education, both at Tarsus and in Jerusalem, was outraged
by the thoughts that assailed him. Always, however, the
gentle tones of Gamaliel impressing the importance that all

truths be examined on their merits, and that God would lead to ultimate truth.

The gushing torrents of the Jordan delta as the snows of high-Hermon melted in the warm sunshine of spring . . . . Was something inside Paul melting too?

As he passed by Caesarea Philippi, did he hear the voice of the ever-living One speak in the quietness: *'And you, Saul of Tarsus, whom do you say that I am?'*?

Of the conversion of Paul, H. V. Morton has written, 'Conversion is often said to be a long, unconscious process of the mind. The subconscious mind goes with hands open to meet conversion, but the conscious mind remains fixed and firm until something happens — some little thing — and a man finds his whole life changed. That seems to have been happening to Paul . . . .'

Beyond the Hermon peaks, and the Golan, the Damascus plain itself — more than 2,000 feet above sea level.

The road to Damascus was straight from there on. And Damascus appeared like an oasis of green in a desert land. The great rivers, of which Namaan had been so proud and which, rightly, he had compared so favourably with the Jordan, had made Damascus an obvious centre of population, commerce and civilization.

It was noon as Paul's party approached. The three accounts of what occurred are as clear as the sky over the Damascus plain. Each is emphatic that there was no thunderstorm or violent wind; no natural explanation of what occurred.

This is what Paul who had received the best education — religious and secular — the age afforded, said to Herod Agrippa II at Caesarea: 'About noon, O King, as I was on the road, I saw a light from heaven, brighter than the sun, blazing round me and my companions. We all fell to the ground, and I heard a voice saying to me in Aramaic, "Saul, Saul, why do you persecute me? It is hard for you to kick against the goads."

'Then I asked, "Who are you, Lord?" '

At that stage Paul had not been committing himself; the word translated 'Lord' here could equally well have been translated 'Sir'. But as he looked up to the centre of light, and before blindness came, he saw nail-scarred hands and feet; and recognized the voice that now spoke to him from the heavens, as the still small voice that had been speaking to his mind since the brutal death of Stephen. Paul knew the answer to his question before it was given.

'"I am Jesus, whom you are persecuting," the Lord replied. "Now get up and stand on your feet. I have appeared to you to appoint you as a servant and as a witness of what you have seen of me and what I will show you. I will rescue you from your own people and from the Gentiles. I am sending you to them to open their eyes and turn them from darkness to light, and from the power of Satan to God, so that you may receive forgiveness of sins and a place among those who are sanctified by faith in me."

'So then, King Agrippa, I was not disobedient to the vision from heaven . . . .'

Paul and the Temple Guard arrived at Damascus in a different humour from that in which they had set out. Paul, blinded, and on foot, was being led by two guards towards the city gates. Among the shambles of the remaining guards, there was amazement, wonder and much quiet discussion.

John Calvin wrote that the 'murderous threats' uttered by Saul as he set off from Jerusalem were 'an allusion to the snorting of wild beasts'. Outside Damascus, God's grace was seen, 'not only in such a cruel wolf being turned into a sheep, but also in assuming the character of a shepherd'.

Modern Damascus is typical of many Arab cities; that which is ancient, though viewed as a source of foreign currency, is inadequately maintained, and quite outshone by the modern buildings piled up above it.

The Via Recta, 'the Street called Straight', was broad, dignified and colonnaded in the first century. It bisected the city from gate to gate. Today the Street of Judas the Damascene, who lodged the Grand Inquisitor come to destroy him, is still the east-west access to the city. But today's 'Street called Straight' is the central souk or market street: no colonnades as in the Greco-Roman period; much corrugated iron.

Christian tradition focuses around the 'house of

Ananias', north of the main souk and the Church of St. Paul. 'Lord,' said Ananias, 'I have heard many reports about this man and all the harm he has done to your saints in Jerusalem.'

The Lord said to Ananias, 'Go! This man is my chosen instrument to carry my name before the Gentiles . . . '.

Following the restoration of his sight and his reception into a bemused Christian community, Paul began to use his finely-honed intellect in the cause of Christ. Trained by Gamaliel, Paul soon had the local rabbis running for cover. Like many rabbis after them, confounded by Paul's arguments, amazed by his Gospel, they appealed to the civil authorities to deal with him. Later, Paul was to tell the Corinthians, perhaps with some amusement, that to preserve his life the local Christians had had to prepare ropes and a fish basket — and lower him down the outside wall of the city so that he could make his escape. Perhaps this is why the most interesting site in today's Damascus is the portion of the first-century wall that remains, overhung in the upper portion, from which it is easy to imagine how Paul's escape was managed.

It is important to secure the assistance of a qualified guide in Damascus. Beneath the modern city, down steep steps, are vaults, byzantine structures, and many of the artefacts of the city of Ananias.

Damascus was not our first exposure to the *khamseen* wind that shortens tempers and, for its duration, makes life extremely uncomfortable. But no one had told us that it could last for more than a week . . . .

Before sunrise, the skies of the Eastern desert had turned as brown as buckram, then slowly darkened, spreading like a bruise and at last releasing the outlines of cloud, giant octaves of ochre massed up from the endless deserts of the Middle East.

We watched everyone shuttering the buildings and, just in time, did so ourselves. Preparations for a hurricane could not have been conducted with greater urgency. But this was no hurricane. A few gusts of air and a thin rain were the forerunners of the darkness that blotted out the light of the sky. Under cover of the darkness the sand wormed in everywhere, as if by magic, appearing in pockets, cupboards and corners of rooms, behind pictures and fingernails, and in the locks themselves. The harsh air dried the membranes of our throats and noses.

From time to time a wind would stir up the whole city, round and round, providing the illusion that everything — trees, minarets, monuments and people — was caught up in an eddying whirlpool of sand, to be poured back into the desert.

Until it ended, and the sea-wind came again, we could not settle to do anything. At the first sign of abatement, contrary to normal practice, we took a taxi to the airport, where we enjoyed a long night's air-conditioning before taking the first flight home.

Away from the *khamseen*, we were free to think again of the greatest conversion of the greatest missionary of the Christ, that shook and still shakes the world. We rejoiced with Paul that Jesus carried a curse on the cross, but not His own; Paul's and everyman's. We rejoiced at the unconditional love of the Saviour, the grace independent of human merit, the righteousness that outweighs human sin and is the one source of our salvation.

Because of its rivers, Damascus has outlived the other ancient cities of the East: Antioch, Ninevah and Babylon. But in the first century Antioch was of infinitely greater importance than Damascus, and had a far vaster population. After Tarsus, it was the place where Paul began to carry out the commission of the noontime voice.

———

Readings
> Acts 9:1-30.
> Acts 23:9-23.
> 2 Corinthians 11:32, 33.

5 ARABIA TO ANTIOCH

Damascus was the terminus of a trade route that began in Arabia and the Horn of Africa. Paul probably took advantage of the cover provided by a camel-borne party of traders as he fled from Damascus. At all events he ended up in Arabia. He wrote to the Galatians, 'I did not consult any man, nor did I go up to Jerusalem to see those who were apostles before I was, but I went immediately into Arabia and after returned to Damascus.' (Galatians 1:16, 17.)

Sensible of his commission to take the Gospel to the wider world, to which the ships of Tarsus set sail and to which the trader-caravans were bound when they passed through the Cilician Gate, Paul knew that he needed time for study. *En route* to Damascus, he had taken on board concepts not dreamt of in the philosophy of Tarsus or the theology of the Jerusalem establishment; he needed time alone — with the Scriptures.

The next three years would appear to have been divided between Arabia and Damascus. Thereafter, in his own account, 'I went up to Jerusalem to get acquainted with Peter and stayed with him fifteen days. I saw none of the other apostles — only James, the Lord's brother . . . . ' (Galatians 1:18, 19.) Despite the elapse of three years, Paul's reputation in Jerusalem as a persecutor was still very much alive. There would have been a number who would have heard the Damascus Road story and decided that it was an unlikely tale. Some had doubtless seen Paul as an infiltrator. We might never have heard of Paul — but for Barnabas. Barnabas was the nickname of a Cypriot called Joseph. Barnabas means 'son of encouragement'; a sobriquet richly deserved by that Levite from Cyprus. Sons of encouragement are big-hearted men, and Barnabas gave Paul the benefit of the doubt. He even persuaded the others to do the same. Paul had found a firm friend.

Paul's fifteen days with Peter would have been ones of intense conversations, and Paul would have had many questions. Peter was one who could testify to 'that which was from the beginning, which we have heard, which we have seen with our eyes, which we have looked at and our hands have touched'. (1 John 1:1.) He had known Jesus personally. It is likely that no one ever debriefed him more thoroughly than did Paul at that time. Nevertheless, since Peter did not grasp as yet the full implications of 'making disciples of all nations' — his dream on the housetop at Joppa was still future — it may be that Paul found his missionary vision somewhat limited.

Whatever transpired, it is likely that Paul derived from Peter the encouragement to begin preaching Christ in the synagogues of the Greek-speaking Jews in Jerusalem, thus continuing the ministry of Stephen. In going back to the places where he was well known, Paul demonstrated immense courage; whether a persecutor or a Gospel champion, Paul was a 100-per-center.

Inevitably, controversy ensued. Paul's murder was soon being plotted. He was smuggled down to the Roman capital, Caesarea, on the coast. From there he sailed home to Tarsus — and more controversy. Indeed, to preach to Jews and Gentiles in his home city might have taken more courage than anything else in his career. But Paul had seen Jesus. Before the glory of that heavenly vision all things paled. In comparison with the purchase price of Calvary's finished redemption, all risk and suffering came cheap. What an immense relief it must have been for an erstwhile Pharisee to turn from his own legalistic righteousness as a method of salvation — and accept salvation by grace through faith in Jesus Christ alone! Like any Pharisee, he had anticipated having to meet the demands of God's infinite holiness by his own endeavours and had been haunted by the dread that there would be some fatal flaw. Learning that by renouncing all he had gained Christ, and by trusting Him, being found in Him, he would possess His flawless righteousness wrought by His obedience unto death — Paul had grasped the freedom of the Gospel. No threat that the mind of men could devise would silence him. By confessing himself incapable of doing good, by identifying himself with the death of Christ, he might come to know the power of His resurrection — and abandon his deadly doings, his strivings, counting all former gains but dross, that he might win Christ and all that Christ could be and do.

What a Gospel!

In the cut and thrust of debate among his own people, and in face of their ostracism, Paul discovered a central truth: religion was relationship, not rules. If spiritual life revolved around anything less than Jesus Christ Himself — doctrines, good works, rules for a holy life — it would inevitably disappoint and fail. But if He was Alpha and Omega; if even in feeble faith, he could look up to Him — *then* he could press on to know Him, counting all things but loss for the excellency of that knowledge.

Thus when Barnabas came to Tarsus to find Paul, to recruit him for the Antioch mission, the Paul that he found was one already bloodied by battle. More important still: a Paul who, scripturally, intellectually and experientially was equipped to lead the major missionary thrust of Christianity. But, for the time being, Paul must play second fiddle . . . .

Josephus Flavius calls Antioch 'the third city of the Empire', after Rome and Alexandria. Cornelius Tacitus in his *Histories* paints a picture of Antioch as a city of fabulous wealth: a source of gold and silver currency and the centre for the manufacture of armaments.

Antioch was the capital of Syria. It was nearer to Tarsus than to Damascus. It was situated fifteen miles up the Orontes River and was hence accessible by boat from the Mediterranean. It guarded the narrow plain that opened to the East towards the Syrian plateau and, itself, was guarded from the south by the massive Mount Silpius, made distinctive by the carving of a faceless human head from its rock.

Populated by Macedons, Greek-speaking Cretans, Orientals from Persia, India and China, indigenous Aramaic speakers and a large community of Jews, it had been the centre of the Seleucid Empire and, by the second century BC, had had a population of half a million. No more appropriate centre could have been found for a world-wide Christian mission. It had been conquered for the Romans by Pompey in 64BC, and Marc Antony and Cleopatra had been married at its Sanctuary of Apollo. Herod the Great had added to its many fine buildings and had paved its main streets with marble. It was called 'Antioch the Beautiful'.

Nicolas of Antioch might well have been the first Christian convert in the city (see Acts 6:5), but, ironically, the real growth of Christianity in Antioch occurred as a direct result of Paul's anti-Christian reign of terror in Jerusalem, prior to his departure for Damascus. That had led to a major migration of Christians from Jerusalem to Antioch. Thus Antioch became the first missionary headquarters of the Christian Church. Indeed, it was in Antioch that the term 'Christian' (*christianoi*), 'the party of Christ' was used for the first time.

The Jerusalem church had sent Barnabas to take charge of an expanding Christian community in Antioch, and Barnabas had remembered Paul and recruited him as his assistant. In addition to Paul and Barnabas there were also Lucius of Cyrene, Manaen, who was a foster brother of the Herod who had executed John the Baptist and mocked Jesus before His crucifixion, and Simon 'Niger', believed to have been 'Simon of Cyrene, the father of Alexander and Rufus', the man pressed by the Romans to carry the cross of Christ.

The Christian team in Antioch were up against it. In that first-century megalopolis there were vast contrasts between rich and poor. And beyond the marbled main streets there were warrens of shanty-town streets where tens of thousands lived on the edge of starvation. The rock-carved human head that dominated the city was believed by the populous to be Charon, a symbol of the spirit being who conveyed dead souls to the underworld. Pleasure was the primary pursuit of the wealthier classes of Antioch. Above all, Antioch had such a reputation for sexual depravity that even ancient Rome frowned upon it! The Grove of Daphne was sequestered in the hills, five miles south of Antioch, and was dominated by a huge statue of the god Apollo. Hundreds of prostitutes were on hand to help any man to worship the goddess of love any way he chose . . . .

Among the hedonists, slaves, criminals, debtors and

degenerates, Paul plunged in, preaching the Gospel of freedom in Jesus Christ. Soon in the Hellenistic gymnasia and sports centres of the city the new faith was being gossiped. One church historian has the rapidly-expanding Christian congregation meeting in Singon Street in the Epiphania district, immediately under the carved head of Charon. Paul's name as a Christian leader was made in Antioch. When the famine referred to in the histories of Gaius Suetonius, Cornelius Tacitus and Josephus Flavius began to ravage Judaea, a collection was made among the relatively wealthy Christians of Antioch and, with Barnabas, Paul was selected to carry the fund to Jerusalem and distribute it among the needy there. They returned accompanied by Barnabas's young nephew, John Mark.

Much later, when the first Christian council occurred in Jerusalem (Acts 15), Paul and Barnabas again went to represent the Christian community in Antioch. The issue before the council was the insistence of the Judaizers that Gentile Christians should undergo the rite of circumcision before acceptance into the community of the faith. To a man like Paul the issue was a simple one: Was one saved by religious rites/works or was one saved by the righteousness of Christ and His blood shed at Calvary? At the Jerusalem Council, Peter insisted that Paul and Barnabas be given a full hearing. James, who apparently acted as chairman, gave the verdict Paul wanted. When Paul and Barnabas returned to Antioch, Judas Barsabbas and Silas went with them.

Following their first visit to Jerusalem on behalf of the Antioch church, Paul and Barnabas planned a 1,400-mile missionary journey on which John Mark would act as their assistant.

When they returned from the Jerusalem council with Judas and Silas, they planned the second missionary journey. That time there was a most regrettable difference of opinion between Paul and Barnabas. On the first missionary journey, Mark had deserted for reasons not given. Paul was determined that he should not accompany them on the second journey. Hence a parting of the ways occurred, with Paul taking Silas, and Barnabas, with a different itinerary, taking

John Mark. At a later time Paul was to relent and acknowledge the great worth of Barnabas's nephew Mark.

When Paul and Barnabas began to evangelize Antioch, the Emperor Gaius (Caligula) ruled in Rome (AD37–41). From the accounts of Gaius Suetonius in *The Twelve Caesars* and Cornelius Tacitus in *The Annals of Imperial Rome*, it is very clear that Caligula was both sexually degenerate to an extreme as yet unparalleled in the history of Rome, and insane. Suetonius writes, 'He established a shrine to himself as god, with priests, the costliest possible victims, and a life-sized golden image, which was dressed every day in clothes identical with those he happened to be wearing . . . . Finally he announced that Jupiter had persuaded him to share his home; and therefore he connected the palace (on the Paletine Hill) with the Capitol by throwing a bridge across the Temple of the god Augustus.'

Caligula also habitually practised incest with his sisters, presided over a brothel in the palace on the Paletine — in which he involved the wives and daughters of senators — and sent hundreds of important men to their deaths on a whim. Inevitably he was assassinated.

As Barnabas and Paul set out for Cyprus on the first missionary journey in the spring of AD47, they were unaware that the relative sanity imposed upon the Empire by the elderly and scholarly Claudius (AD41–54) would significantly assist in the success of their missionary endeavours. Four years earlier Claudius had conquered Britain, an island on the mist-shrouded extremity of the world which had been part of the Roman network of trade since Julius Caesar had visited it three generations previously.

Readings
> Galatians 1:11-2:1.
> Acts 12:24-13:3.
> Galatians 5:1-6.

6   CYPRUS: PARADISE ISLAND

The low halo of sun-over-sea reflected a ruddy, healthy glow on the faces of the outdoor diners at the waterfront restaurants.

The hills turned from rouge to purple in the time it took us to take the coast road from Paphos for the lighthouse. The sea was the colour of wine, glittering with what looked like the sweepings of broken glass.

Before the sun-halo had quite disappeared, we saw, ahead of us, the silhouette of a scene straight out of Scripture. A shepherd was leading his sheep along the coast path towards a valley flooded with heavy shadow. As he walked, he talked to the sheep. At times he was calling stragglers by name. Mostly, he was talking to them as if they were friends. They were long-necked Levantine sheep with ribs like radiators, and responded to the voice of the man who led them.

Since he was unaware that we were approaching from behind, we took care not to startle either the man or his animals. 'Do you speak English?' we asked. With an old-fashioned deference he told us he did; it had been learned in school. He was, it appeared, caring for the sheep that belonged to his aged mother. The names he had for each of them related to the nearest saint's day to the date of their birth. Close up we could see that the man, though by no means old, had the leathery skin of one exposed to the year-long elements. Mostly, he said, he slept beside his sheep because of the danger from foxes and wild dogs.

We had found our doorway to the Cyprus of Barnabas, Paul and Mark. It was possible to escape the Cyprus of the tourist. And, having escaped it, we did not have occasion to revisit it until we took the flight home. At one point we had to confront political difficulties of which Paul would have been innocent. We were not permitted to visit Salamis — where the missionary party had landed — because it was in the Turkish-occupied part of the island. Once again we contrasted the petty nationalisms of our day with the far-flung Empire within which Paul worked. It was surely a paradox that, though so rotten at its heart, the Roman Empire blessed the first-century world with roads, culture, political stability and freedom of movement: an almost ideal environment for the spread of the Christian Gospel.

We made the most of Paphos, in Paul's day the seat of the Roman proconsul Sergius Paullus. The missionary party had travelled through the whole island before they reached Paphos on the southern coast. In some places they might have encountered small Christian communities (Acts 11:19). They preached the Gospel wherever they went, principally perhaps in the synagogues. As a Cypriot, Barnabas had a strong feeling for his own people and was to return to Cyprus to continue the Christian mission when Paul left Antioch on his second missionary journey.

Approaching Paphos along the southern coastline, Paul and Barnabas would have walked round the bay where, according to Homer's tale, the goddess of love, Aphrodite, emerged from the spuming foam of the Mediterranean. They would have given a wide berth to her famous temple; there, as at Daphne near Antioch, prostitution counted for religious devotion.

Before they reached the Roman city of Paphos and its great harbour, they encountered a practitioner of occult arts, Bar-Jesus or Elymas (the sorcerer). The sorcerer was part of the court of Sergius Paullus.

Hearing of the arrival in Paphos of the missionary party, 'the proconsul, an intelligent man, sent for Barnabas and Saul because he wanted to hear the word of God'. That was the cue for the sorcerer to emerge in his proper colours. Like the Druids who opposed the coming of Celtic Christianity to the British Isles, Elymas did all he could to influence the mind of the proconsul against the ambassadors of Christ.

It was at the palace of the proconsul that, perhaps for the first time, Paul took the initiative. The party had arrived on Cyprus as 'Barnabas and Saul'; they were to leave as 'Paul and Barnabas'. In front of everyone, Paul denounced Elymas and the diabolic source from which his powers came. Elymas was temporarily blinded. That gave Paul the opportunity to expound the Gospel to Sergius Paullus. As a result, the Roman proconsul became the first ruler of any country to commit himself to the cause of Christ.

At one time the accuracy of Luke, author of Acts, in describing Sergius Paullus as 'a proconsul' was questioned. The critics said that Cyprus belonged to the Senate, not the Emperor, and hence would have had a 'legate', not a proconsul. Manuscript and archaeological discoveries have completely confounded this line of argument and, as in other matters, upheld the reputation of Luke as a meticulously accurate historian. Since Pliny the Elder cites Sergius Paullus as an authority in his own *Natural History*, we may also deduce that the proconsul was an authority in the field of science. It is, perhaps, surprising that so important a lay Christian should have had such a brief, cameo appearance in the record of the Acts. Archaeological discoveries made by Sir William Ramsay in Turkey in 1912 provided more information about the contribution of Sergius Paullus to the Christian story. From an unearthed inscription it would appear that the conversion of the proconsul of Cyprus led to a conflict within his own family. The upshot of the conflict was that his daughter became a Christian, whereas his son, later governor of Galatia, remained arrogantly pagan.

Our visit to the excavations known as the 'House of Dionysos' gave us a mental picture of what the palace of Sergius Paullus must have looked like. The villa enclosed 2,000 square metres, 556 square metres of which were covered with an incredibly beautiful mosaic which, thanks to the archaeologists, we were still able to appreciate. As we approached the site it was the mosaic that first caught our attention; from a distance, it looked like a beautifully-woven Persian carpet. The archaeologists believe it to be the best-preserved mosaic in the world. Work is still going on on this site, high on a hill overlooking the old harbour where the palace of the proconsul would have been. Whether this *was*, in fact, the palace of the proconsul at the time of Paul is debatable. That it existed at the time of Paul is, however, beyond question.

Another archaeological site, somewhat out of the way but still within walking distance of Paphos, contains the ruins of a massive byzantine cathedral dedicated to St. Kyriaki Chrysopolitissa. Among the ruins of this cathedral is what is known as 'St. Paul's Pillar'. This marble column, approximately ten feet tall, is the subject of an ancient local legend. Everyone to whom we spoke was convinced that this was the pillar to which the apostle Paul was tied to receive one of his 'two score save one' lashings. Since Paul simply mentions his whippings in a long list of other afflictions he had suffered for Christ, and since Luke does not record where those whippings occurred, it is not entirely impossible that one took place on Cyprus. It must be recalled that most of the missionary work done on Cyprus was among the Jews and that the conversion of Sergius Paullus came not long before the departure of the missionaries for Galatia. Hence the legend cannot be dismissed out of hand.

On the edge of the byzantine ruins is a church now shared by Anglicans and Roman Catholics.

One night when the Mediterranean moon was a great whiteness like a round furnace door, when the sands appeared like ground silver and the sea moved in solid brightness coming towards them, we sat outside a restaurant and talked history with some savants of the local population. We came, they told us, from a country whose history was little longer than 2,000 years. They came from an island, they said, whose recorded history stretched back at least 6,000 years. In common with Greek Cypriots we met elsewhere, we found that our evening friends had a habit of speaking of the figures of ancient history, such as Philip the Macedon and Alexander the Great, as if they were near-contemporaries. At one instant they could be justifying Greek possession of the island by reference to the conquests of Alexander and, in the next instant, blaming us for letting the Turks in during the century when Cyprus was a British possession (needless to say, we denied all personal responsibility!).

Cypriot claims to a long history are not open to question.

Similarly, the discovery of Mycenaean pottery enables us to date Greek settlement of cities like Salamis and Paphos to a period as distant as 1200BC. The Greeks were on Cyprus before Israel had its first king.

For Christian history the Tombs of the Kings have considerable significance. These tombs, situated half way between the harbour and the new town, are very impressive, even to the modern eye; hewn out of rock, they feature imposing pillars and mysterious steps disappearing down into the dark. While these tombs date from a period three centuries before Christ, their Christian credentials arise from the fact that, like the catacombs, they were used as hiding places for early Christians under persecution.

Off the main road into Kato Paphos is the Catacomb of St. Solomoni. This catacomb takes the form of underground caves that lead to a central courtyard. They date from the Hellenistic period and were certainly part of the Cypriot scene when Paul and Barnabas passed by on the road above. The association with St. Solomoni arose when Roman soldiers, at that time persecuting the Christians, pursued Solomoni and her seven sons into the caves and, rather than flushing them out, chose to entomb them there. An archaeological examination of the caves turns up evidence that they were used both for Christian worship and as a Christian retreat in the face of persecution. The names of crusaders are etched into the walls of the Catacomb. An incredibly gnarled old tree is growing out of it. There is an ancient belief that a handkerchief tied on this tree will act as a cure for disease. In consequence the branches of the tree are covered with handkerchiefs.

Other cities on the south coast of Cyprus have blaring discotheques, hideous hotels and other concessions to the tourist industry. Paphos does not. It does, however, have an incredible number of restaurants and a good many tavernas. There is a great deal of warmth and friendliness. An evening stroll around the harbour can mean a score of invitations to eat in the various restaurants. The Greek invitation has charm — perhaps backed up by an offer of free drinks — but not the irritating persistence we are accustomed to encounter elsewhere in the Levant.

One soft, early-July evening, after a blisteringly hot day, as a milk-warm wind wafted off the Mediterranean, we received an invitation with a difference. It was to take a ride in a glass-bottomed boat. Evening rides are unusual, but the heat had been against the boatman in the daytime and he had a family to keep. He provided us with a magical experience. Despite the fluorescent blue that hangs to the seaweed and represents modern-day pollution, there is much to be seen of incredible beauty. Turtles can live to be 120 years old, but are very vulnerable to predators. Hence to examine a turtle reserve from a glass-bottomed boat somehow seemed to be the perfect end to our final day on an idyllic island.

After Cyprus, there is no more mention of 'Saul', only of 'Paul'. As the 'Paul and Barnabas' team crossed from Paphos to Perga in Pamphylia *en route* to Galatia, they probably had more than a shrewd suspicion that the real rigours of the journey were about to begin. That might have been the reason for Mark's desertion.

A by-no-means contemporary description of Paul has him as a feeble, bow-legged figure with a bald head. Every icon we have ever seen of Paul has featured the latter characteristic. The sheer physical exertion of foot-slogging through tough terrain over long distances through mountains, valleys and plateaux, with long miles between settlements surely gives the lie to the 'feeble, bow-legged' part of the description. Aside from the brutality of the treatment they were to receive, the fact that they stayed that rigorous course pays tribute to the mental, physical and spiritual strength of Barnabas and Paul. That is not to say that Paul had no physical weakness . . . .

But as he did the distance between Antioch-in-Pisidia to Iconium, and from Lystra to Derbe — and back, it speaks volumes for the power of the 'heavenly vision' in the purpose of Paul. 'This one thing I do,' Paul was to write about his pursuit of spiritual maturity; but the same single-mindedness was brought to the prosecution of his mission, regardless of

Nafplio, once the Greek capital, is an excellent centre from which to visit the Pauline and ancient sites of Greece.

Caesarea was the Roman capital of Palestine. Built by Herod the Great, it was the base from which governors like Pontius Pilate, Felix and Festus sought to govern a turbulent province. Paul passed through Caesarea on a number of occasions, and was imprisoned there for two years. Caesarea's excavation began in 1956. This was a Roman aqueduct that brought water to the Caesarea of Paul's day.

Corinth was a vast, cosmopolitan population centre in the ancient world. Here Paul encountered his greatest challenge. Lechaion Road, pictured, leads to the acropolis from which prostitute priestesses came down to ply their trade in the first century.

Assos, a tiny port city twenty miles south-east of Troas, was where Paul embarked for Jerusalem at the end of his third missionary journey.

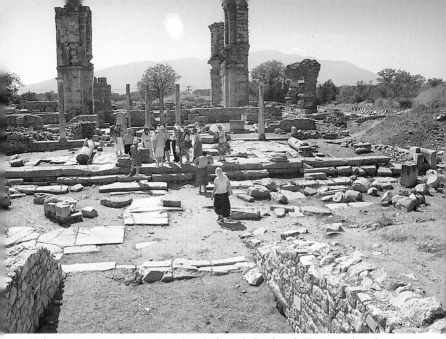

Philippi was a Roman garrison town. Here Paul preached and, with Silas, was whipped and imprisoned. Excavations have revealed a Greek, as well as a Roman city. Here the ruins of a Byzantine church are viewed across the agora.

Lydia's church. In the nearby river Paul baptized those who accepted Christ at Philippi. Among them was Lydia.

Neapolis (modern Kavala) was Paul's port of entry into Europe. This Roman aqueduct was in use until the early twentieth century.

Paul came to Neapolis having received a vision in Troas. Modern Kavala is a beautiful port city and holiday centre. From Neapolis Paul struck out on the Egnatian Way to Philippi and Thessalonica.

Delphi's agora, with the Temple of Apollo in the background and, high above, the stadium where the games were held.

The Metéora, topped by monasteries, are among the sites not to be missed.

Delphi is one of the most beautiful sites in Greece. In the Temple of Apollo, the ruins of which are seen here, the 'Oracle' dispensed occult 'wisdom' to all comers — Caesars, generals, senators, philosophers.

Mount Olympus, viewed from Litohoro. The ancients believed this mountain to be the home of the gods.

Mars Hill, just below the Parthenon, Athens, where Paul preached to the philosophers.

The Odeion of Herodes Atticus, still in use, was one of the sites Paul would have viewed in Athens.

The Parthenon dominates Athens. It has occupied the rock platform of the acropolis since more than four centuries before Paul's visit.

circumstances, through sun and storm, through misrepresentation to ecstasy.

It was in Galatia that the mission to the Gentiles got going in earnest. Hence it was in Galatia that the venom of both Jews and Judaizers really broke loose. Not only Paul but his Gospel drew heavy fire. But there was something in Paul that the hatred of the Jews could not touch, that the fickleness of the crowds could not daunt, that the hailstorm of stones at Lystra could not budge. It was the 'heavenly vision' to name the name of Christ where it had never been named before; and to introduce men and women, regardless of religion, race or class, to the Gospel that brought freedom, assurance, peace, joy — and eternity. That was what brought Paul round from his death-swoon at Lystra, that caused him to struggle on from city to city — and then to retrace his steps confirming his converts in the faith. An amphitheatre of raging fanatics or a courtful of dignitaries with the high, low and middle justice at their disposal did not move Paul.

But his vision was fed. There were high tides of revelation and vision in that Galatian adventure (see 2 Corinthians 12:1) that none of the several languages Paul had at his disposal possessed vocabulary to describe (verse 4). Nevertheless, through the perils of robbers, of waters, of mountain passes and of violent crowds, Paul *was* in with a physical handicap. He called it a 'thorn in the flesh'; and it had nothing to do with bow legs! The word Paul used to describe it is 'a stake' as if he were impaled; he is talking real, constant pain. It says something for him that he refused to name the ailment; that refusal also enables us to identify our 'thorns in the flesh' with his. The balance of probability points to an eye problem, not surprising in one who had spent years poring over manuscripts. But it must have been something more than 'weak eyes'; there is the pain to account for.

It was during that first journey that, on three separate occasions, Paul pleaded to be delivered from his affliction. Perhaps the keen blast that swept through the mountain plateau on which Antioch-in-Pisidia stood had aggravated the condition. At all events, he not only learned to live with the answer he received, but found in that answer life's sole secret: 'My grace is sufficient for thee!'

Paul was not Paul because he could slay the world with his jawbone!

———

Readings
  Acts 13:1-12.
  2 Corinthians 11:24-28.
  2 Corinthians 12:7-9.

7 FROM ISTANBUL TO GALATIA

An earthquake hit Istanbul the day we landed. It registered 6.5 on the Richter scale. But it was the least of our inconveniences. In England there had been taxis that didn't turn up, a last-minute mad dash to catch a train, a sardine-packed one-and-a-half-hour stand peering through dirty windows at England's winter wonderland. As we journeyed towards Kings Cross, the train jerking its arthritic way over frozen points, we sliced through gorse-lined cuttings heavy with snow and rumbled over bridges that gave us glimpses of empty motorways . . . .

Security at 'Heathrow was stricter than we had ever known it. 'There *is* a war on,' somebody reminded us. 'Nobody should be flying to Turkey . . . . Americans are not flying *anywhere.*' We had had all this, and more, from friends and relations. The war, in fact, was part of the reason for our journey. Airlines were flying more than half empty; Turkey was full of empty four-star hotels, and Peltours had decided to offer a Pauline-sites-in-Turkey trip at a ridiculous, knock-down price. In theory the trip was for hardy clergy who would, come peace and summer, lead their flocks on more expensive tours around the same sites (not that Peltours are ever *that* expensive).

Right until the last minute, the escalation of the Gulf War and the use by the Allies of Turkish air bases had threatened to cancel our trip. In the event, as we discovered at Heathrow, the original complement had gone down from twenty-five to fifteen. Peltours could not afford to send one of their own people with us, so we were at the tender mercies of a parson from Paignton. Fortunately, Turkish government regulations required us to have a qualified Turkish guide. Bilal was to prove priceless.

As we made friends with our thirteen fellow travellers in the slow-moving Heathrow queues, we discovered that, like us, they had wearied of saturation media coverage of Saddam Hussein's war. Once in Turkey we found that the war was easily ignored. Apart from bombers over Tarsus and the closure, for security reasons, of Topkapi — the ancient residence of the Sultans built over the site of Constantine's imperial palace — it did not impinge at all.

Take-off was one hour late; the airport was covered with snow and there was ice on the runway. As the Turkish Airlines jet, less than a third full, took off into a snowstorm, we caught the Lancashire cadences of the Catholic priest on the seat behind. 'It's easy to get holy water these days. Just fill a kettle and boil the Hell out of it.' · We had made the acquaintance of septuagenarian Bill Fry and his brother-in-law Con. Though Bill's rotund amplitude would slow down many of our walks, his wit and wisdom would warm us whatever the temperature. The Famous Fifteen comprised Anglicans (High, Broad and Low), one Church of Scotland minister from Dalbeattie, a Free Presbyterian minister and his wife from Newtownards and a lovable London Methodist youth minister called Steve.

Peltours had planned the operation like the Normandy invasion, though with more paperwork! But even they had not thought to prepare us for one small aspect of Turkish travel. Entrées, whether labelled 'beef', 'chicken', or anything else for that matter are invariably mutton. Those with an aversion to mutton or meat were in with a handicap. This was true throughout our travels in Turkey.

As we landed, nightfall had reduced Istanbul's incredible skyline to bas-reliefs upon a screen of gold and violet.

'East is east and west is west and ne'er the twain shall meet . . . '; but there *is* a place where east meets west . . . . The floodlit darkness of this most marvellous and mysterious of cities revealed more than enough to whet everyone's appetite. Night lay over the streets like velvet strips, but the lighted tips of the minarets rose above it on their slender, invisible stalks. Overcome by the soft, dazed evening air, we wanted to stay in this first and last city in Europe. The lights made mosques and bridges and the multi-coloured flat waters of the Sea of Marmara, the Golden Horn and the Bosphorus, that interspersed the city, evoke Constantinople, even Byzantium, as well as Istanbul.

But some uniformed official ordered us and our luggage aboard a bus. Then, before we knew it, we were packed into an ancient DC9 and juddering through the night sky to Izmir. 'Tomorrow', said Bilal, 'you have long journey. Yes?' Bilal was not given to overstatement.

In their mercy, the tour company had broken up the journey by coach from Izmir (Smyrna) to Perga, where Paul and Barnabas landed in Asia Minor. The breaks and stopovers helped us catch a glimpse of the Hellenistic centres from which the culture of the Roman period derived.

First stop, **Priene**, where Alexander the Great spent more than a year. On this occasion, with Bill Fry, I formed the *derriere-guard* of the party. Out of earshot of Bilal's 'little informations' I benefited from the father's personal perceptions. Thanks to the archaeologist there is much to see of this ancient Greek city. Enough, in fact, to conjure up a colourful picture of how life would have been when this was a prosperous, new, port city, when Alexander rode into town in 334BC. The well-excavated Temple of Athena was built at the initiative of Alexander. 'Interesting,' Bill Fry was muttering. 'These pagan temples were built to house a god, not as a place for people to come and worship the god. Just look at these vast columns and try to imagine the scale of the place . . . . All this just for the benefit of a statue!'

From the temple we managed to visit a theatre, a council chamber with seating for 640 and the altar of Dionysius.

From Priene our coach took us to **Didyma**. The ruins of this ancient Greek city were, if anything, even more impressive. Most imposing of all was the Temple of Apollo, the third largest structure in the Hellenic world, outdone only slightly by the Temple of Artemis in Ephesus. Not far from Miletus where Paul was to address the Ephesian elders, Didyma was a centre of superstition; the Oracle of Apollo rivalled the Oracle at Delphi.

Bilal was especially proud to show us around the site

of **Aphrodisias**. This impressive site had been excavated by a Turkish professor who had recently died and been interred on the site. Bilal proudly gathered the group together so that the vast stadium burst upon our collective view at the same instant. It was truly awesome, intact, and had been used for chariot racing. It is an example of what other stadia (theatres), long since decayed, would have looked like.

We had noticed that archaeological sites brought Bilal to life. He would have taken us to more had we not reminded him that we were, after all, seeking to tread in the footsteps of the apostle Paul. However, as he was not slow to remind us, the excavations of these ancient cities represent the best illustrations of what the Hellenistic cities Paul evangelized would have been like.

At last we reached **Perga** on the coast of ancient Pamphylia, where Paul commenced the arduous mainland leg of his first missionary journey. By then in his late 40s, Paul had a journey ahead of him that would have broken many a younger man. Perga, in the Gulf of Attalia, was an unhealthy walled city beneath an imposing acropolis. The road he took inland, up-mountain, would have been steeper than any he had known before. Sudden heavy snow storms were *our* main hazard; but as Paul took the Roman pass round the hairpin bends between the mountains, heat is likely to have been *his* problem. Heat, interspersed with drenching storms that created raging torrents through the gullies in the rock. Later he would write, in his second letter to his friends in Corinth (11:26, 27), 'I have been in danger from rivers, in danger from bandits . . . ; I have laboured and toiled and have often gone without sleep; I have known hunger and thirst and have often gone without food; I have been cold and naked.' That was the toughest assignment of Paul's life. The pressure would have been all the greater since Paul and Barnabas no longer had young John Mark to help with the fetching and carrying.

Beyond the mountains, Paul and Barnabas entered the province of Galatia that covered much of central Anatolia. Their first port of call, **Pisidian Antioch** (now Yalvac), had been refortified and partially rebuilt in the reign of Augustus. Great arches, as magnificent as those in Rome, commemorated the achievements of Augustus, and a glistening white marble temple stood in his honour.

Paul made for the Jewish community and, on the Sabbath, preached in the synagogue. Addressing Gentile converts to Judaism, as well as the Jews, in familiar pattern, Paul told the history of Israel and demonstrated how it all culminated in the death and resurrection of Jesus the Messiah.

Excitement spread, especially among the Gentile converts. Nevertheless, it must have been the synagogue authorities who invited Paul and Barnabas 'to speak further about these things on the next Sabbath'. (Acts 13:42.) The impact of the Gospel had been such that, on the next Sabbath, 'almost the whole city gathered to hear the word of the Lord'. (Verse 44.) That the Jewish authorities could not handle. It was almost certainly in Pisidian Antioch that Paul received one of his three beatings with the rods of Roman lictors. They were expelled from the city. Time for discouragement? 'The disciples were filled with joy and with the Holy Spirit.' (Verse 52.)

Ahead of the two men was the ninety-mile walk between the Taurus and Sultan mountain ranges to **Iconium** (modern name, Konya). More than once *we* thought that we might have to turn back — because of snowstorms. The rumour was also circulating that the Turkish authorities might disapprove of the direction of our journey; they were keen to keep everyone as far away as possible from those aerodromes from which the onslaught on Baghdad was being launched.

Paul's perils were likely to have been, as before, the blistering heat of high summer and equally merciless bandits. Nevertheless, the following Sabbath found Paul and Barnabas preaching the Gospel in one of the Iconium synagogues. 'There they spoke so effectively that a great number of Jews and Gentiles believed.' (Acts 14:1.) But the pattern established in Antioch was repeated; the pharisaical Jews resented the success of the Gospel preachers and conspired to destroy them. At Iconium the population was divided; some for the Pharisees, some for the Gospel missionaries. They would appear to have faced both a mob stirred up by the Pharisees — and a conspiracy on the part of the establishment Jews, to have them stoned. Discretion seemed the better part of valour and they fled towards Lystra.

In Antioch, nothing remained of the city Paul would have seen except, for a fairly typical Roman aqueduct. In the first century, Iconium was insignificant by comparison with its neighbours, Antioch and Lystra, two garrison cities. But at least it had been on the Roman road and, though not a Roman centre, it might well have been populous. It would appear that Paul and Barnabas wintered there. Little or nothing remains of the city they knew. In present-day Iconium (Konya) there are mosques and palaces dating from between the eleventh and fourteenth centuries. But as for Greek Iconium, it has yet to be excavated from beneath the medieval city that covers it.

The experience of the two missionaries in **Lystra** (Zostera) differed from the pattern in the previous two cities. Paul and Barnabas were mistaken for gods! There was a legend in Lystra that Zeus and Hermes had once come to earth incognito. No one had offered them hospitality except two old peasants, Philemon and his wife Baucis. As a result, the gods had wiped out the entire population — except the two peasants. Hence, as soon as the population witnessed Paul and Barnabas's healing the sick, they were determined not to make the same mistake as their ancestors. In vain Paul and Barnabas insisted that they were Gospel preachers, not gods.

Eventually, however, the light dawned on the minds of the enthusiastic pagans. What helped it to dawn was the arrival in Lystra of pharisaical Jews from Antioch and Iconium. The fickle crowd was won over. Paul was stoned; perhaps he thought of Stephen and prayed Stephen's prayer. His body was slung outside the city for dead. But he had been long enough in Lystra to have made converts. They gathered round him, nursed him overnight and, at first light, saw him off with Barnabas on the sixty-mile trek to Derbe. Not long after, Paul wrote, 'I bear on my body the marks of Jesus.' (Galatians 6:17.)

Howling winds and driving snow served to impair our investigation of the archaeological sites of ancient Lystra at Zostera, near Hatunsaray. The same hazards prevented us

from finding the site of **Derbe** at all, though the driver —
called 'Capitan' by Bilal — assured us that we were as near to
the site as any of his previous parties had been and that it
was 'certainly very near the Turkish town of Kerti Huyuk'.

John Wesley, from experience, once advised, 'Always look
a mob in the face.' That would appear to have been Paul's
attitude too. Having 'preached the good news' in Derbe 'and
won a large number of disciples', the missionaries set off
back to Lystra, Iconium and Antioch to strengthen the congregations of believers they had already established there.
That course of action seems all the more courageous when we
consider that only the Cilician Gates, and a walk on a familiar, much-frequented road, separated Paul from his home
town of Tarsus.

As we drove on to Tarsus, we thought of the long, weary
journey Paul and Barnabas took as they retraced their steps
in the opposite direction. Then we thought of the discouragement that awaited them when, after a sea journey from Perga
to Seleucia, they arrived back at home base in Antioch. To
the believers in the other Antioch, in Iconium, in Lystra, and
in Derbe, Paul was soon writing, 'You foolish Galatians!
Who has bewitched you?' Something had gone terribly
wrong.

Readings

Acts 13:13-14:28.

Note. For the purposes of this book the author accepts the arguments of modern scholars that the cities visited by Paul in central Asia
Minor were, at the time of his missionary journeys, in South Galatia,
and that the Letter to the Galatians was written to them. See F. F.
Bruce, *The Epistle to the Galatians: A Commentary on the Greek Text*
(1982), pages 43 *et seq*; J. R. W. Stott, *The Message of Acts* (1990),
pages 222, 233, 242-244.

8 EPHESUS TO LAODICEA

The Antioch church was caught up in a controversy when Paul and Barnabas arrived back in the late summer of AD48. The main opposition they had encountered in Galatia had been from pharisaical Jews. In Antioch they discovered that a party of Christians had been disrupting the congregation. After a short time, information came to hand that Christian Pharisees — a sort of 'Law Party' — had also been unsettling the congregations Paul had left behind in Galatia. Their method had been infiltration (Galatians 2:4).

In Antioch, Paul encountered the Law Party head on.

Soon he had written a hard-hitting letter to be read out in each of the Galatian churches.

This first Christian heresy struck at the very heart of the Gospel. Paul was much exercised. The Law Party preached 'a different gospel — which is really no gospel at all' (Galatians 1:6, 7). The authentic Gospel, Paul reminded the Galatians, was salvation by grace through faith in Jesus Christ alone. The Law Party, in the words of John Stott, taught 'that faith in Jesus was not enough, not sufficient for salvation: they must add to faith, circumcision, and to circumcision, observance of the law'. Was man saved by faith in Christ or by his own track record — which?

That was the issue that led to the attendance of Paul and Barnabas at the Jerusalem Council. Soon, armed with the decision of the Council, Paul returned to Antioch. Then, as soon as weather permitted, with Silas Paul set out by the shortest route to Galatia — through the Cilician Gate. In the congregations at **Derbe, Iconium, Lystra** and **Pisidian Antioch**, Paul reinforced the message of the letter to the Galatians: 'You who are trying to be justified by law have been alienated from Christ; you have fallen away from grace . . . . For in Christ Jesus neither circumcision nor uncircumcision has any value. The only thing that counts is faith expressing itself through love.' (Galatians 5:4, 6.)

In Lystra, Paul recruited young Timothy and set off through Mysia to Troas on the Aegean.

It is thought that Paul commenced his second missionary

journey in April AD50. His first journey had involved him in well in excess of a thousand miles of walking. His second journey took him from one extremity of Anatolia to the other, and from thence into Europe. We travelled this route by coach and, given the vast distances involved, and despite our four-star billets, considered that we had merited a rest before crossing back into Europe. Greece was, in any event, not on our itinerary.

Our — *we* felt — much-needed R and R was two days in Kusadasi, even in winter an incredibly beautiful Turkish seaside resort. Peltours had chosen it because of its proximity to Ephesus.

On his second missionary journey Paul was guided past the seven-cities centre of population, trade and culture — directly to Europe. We had chosen to spend our last eight days in Paul's Asia Minor on a whistle-stop tour of the seven churches. On his third journey Paul would spend between two and three years in the great port city of **Ephesus**. He would write a letter to the Christians in Colossae, another population centre in the region, and in it express concern for believers in nearby **Laodicea** (Colossians 2:1). By the last decade of the first century, Ephesus would be the largest Christian centre in Asia Minor. Its bishop, John, would write letters to each of the seven churches under his supervision (Revelation 2 and 3), and would do so from his lonely place of exile on the Isle of Patmos.

Our seven-cities tour began in Paul's Ephesus.

Long before dawn I was boning up on Ephesus on the balcony of our Kusadasi hotel. Gazing over the Mediterranean, it seemed to me that the edges of the darkness trembled and, here and there, the horizon flickered with light from a distant storm's sheet-lightning. The sea lapping below, the wind knuckling the palms, I watched the storm approach. While we ate breakfast, the whole region received a drenching.

Hence our party of fifteen picked its way around puddles as it entered the site of Ephesus. In the summer the ancient paved streets of this vast, well-excavated archaeological site are crammed with visitors. The storm passed; a warm sun beamed from a cloudless sky — and we enjoyed the entire city to ourselves!

Ephesus, according to Shakespeare, was full of 'dark-working sorcerers that changed the mind'. The Ephesus that became the biggest Christian centre in Asia Minor was also a centre for the study of all aspects of the occult. Some time after his lengthy stay, and despite the bonfire of occult paraphernalia (Acts 19:19), Paul still felt it necessary to remind the Ephesians that 'our fight is not against any physical enemy: it is against organizations and powers that are spiritual. We are up against the unseen power that controls this dark world, and spiritual agents from the very headquarters of evil.' (Ephesians 6:12, 13, Phillips.) In this same epistle, some say Paul's finest, he expressed the very essence of the Gospel in all its sublime simplicity: 'It is by grace you have been saved, through faith — and this not from yourselves, it is the gift of God — not by works, so that no one can boast.' (Ephesians 2:8, 9.)

We walked down ancient Curetes Street past Hadrian's temple, the incredibly beautiful mosaic pavement to our left. Ahead was the imposing façade of the Library of Celsus. With temperatures equivalent to those of an English summer day, we entered into the atmosphere of this Pauline place.

The grand theatre that seats 24,000 people is in a remarkable state of repair, its acoustics brilliant. At each site one of us would take a turn to read the relevant Scriptures. In this theatre that took thirty years to build, and in which Paul doubtless preached, I chose to sit on the farthest outer perimeter. Nevertheless, I had no difficulty whatever in hearing every word that Bill Fry read far down below in the centre. The account of Paul's conflict with the followers of 'Artemis of the Ephesians' and the ensuing riot came alive as we sat *in situ*.

From my perch at the top of the Grand Theatre I could see the Arcadian Way, the main thoroughfare of Greco-Roman Ephesus, eleven metres wide, marble-paved and colonnaded, that led to the place where the harbour had once been. Over the centuries not only has the harbour been silted up, but the whole valley almost up to the horizon! Nevertheless, I found it easy to imagine the riot fomented by the silversmiths who made their living crafting miniatures of Artemis. 'The whole city was in an uproar. The people seized Gaius and Aristarchus, Paul's travelling companions' (presumably Paul's Roman citizenship prevented them from seizing him) 'and rushed as one man into the theatre. Paul wanted to appear before the crowd, ... Even some of the officials of the province, friends of Paul, sent him a message begging him not to venture into the theatre. . . . ' (Acts 19:28-31.)

The Ephesus Paul visited was dominated by the Temple of Artemis (Greek) or Diana (Latin). Among the seven wonders of the ancient world, the temple was four times the size of the Parthenon of Athens. Each of its 127 marble pillars was the gift of a king. It was largely destroyed when the Goths sacked Ephesus in AD263. The marvel is that such a magnificent structure could vanish. Today one pillar remains near the basilica of St. John. Others were used in the construction of the Hagia Sophia in Istanbul.

Paul spent between two and three years in Ephesus. He taught daily in the lecture-room of a Gentile schoolmaster nicknamed Tyrannus. Although he was allowed only the siesta hours of noon to 4pm, when it was too hot to study, the impact of his ministry was great. In the Message to the Ephesian Church (Revelation 2:1-7), the Risen Christ would commend them for their perseverance and intolerance of occult forces; adding, with a note of sadness, 'You have forsaken your first love.'

No student of Scripture or antiquity will visit Ephesus and be disappointed. Much of what is not to be found in this most impressive of all archaeological sites is in the museum in the nearby Turkish city of Selçuk. Of obvious interest is the multi-breasted Artemis of the Ephesians.

When, on the following morning, we left Kusadasi behind for the last time, the wind, though warm, evoked thoughts of storms at sea as it whipped the Mediterranean into a frenzy. When we stumbled from our coach at **Miletus** the wind was

blowing at hurricane force. Bilal's 'little informations' were
blown away, unheard. The attempt to read the story of how
Paul, at the end of his third missionary journey, stopped off
at Miletus to address the Ephesian elders was abandoned.

From Miletus, Capitan aimed the coach up the long valley
that follows the course of the River Meander towards
Laodicea.

We passed acres of orange orchards, the trees bent by the
sea-borne wind. As we made our way across flatlands
towards distant mountains, the force of the wind abated a
little and we watched baggy-trousered Turkish women 'reap-
ing' the orange harvest. Occasionally there were donkey carts
piled high with oranges. As we passed through the towns we
saw boxes of oranges being loaded on lorries. In these towns
the Islamic Revolution was low-key. The minarets were
crumbling, inconspicuous.

The coach was climbing. The road, still lined with sacks
of oranges, was sunk beneath a range of curious, pointed
mountains. By now the Meander criss-crossed beneath the
road and, occasionally, we caught sight of shepherds herding
black sheep and long-haired, black goats.

Before midnight, the scene lit only by the snows that lay
everywhere, we entered the mountain town of Pamukkale. It
was cold; we were high up in the mountain range.

As we unpacked in our ultra-modern, motel-type room,
all the lights went out. A midnight storm was boiling down
the mountain and the power lines were affected. All night, in
beds covered by rugs made from the long hair of the black
goats of the region, we struggled to keep warm, watched the
lightning slashing through the sky in angry stabs and listened
to the thunder as it echoed round the mountains, and the rain
as it bashed against the walls.

Next morning, following a leisurely breakfast, we walked
up to **Hierapolis**. I was totally unprepared for the visual
impact. Hierapolis is a city built on a mountainside of
calcified rock. From a distance it looks like snow. It gleams
like a glacier and is visible from the site of Colossae, twelve
miles distant. Walking over the great white surfaces,
sometimes terraced, sometimes bevelled, gave us a curious

sensation. Above the city was a series of hot volcanic springs reaching a temperature of 98 degrees Celsius. By the time the lime-charged water poured through the gullies and over the terraces of Hierapolis, temperatures had fallen significantly. When the water reached Laodicea, down mountain, by way of channels and aqueducts, it was lukewarm . . . .

There is a theatre at **Laodicea**, and the ruins of a byzantine church. Huddling under the arches to get out of the rain I tried to give the party some background on this remarkable city to which the Risen Christ delivered such a strident message (Revelation 3:14-22). Right from the beginning of the expedition I had known that Laodicea was the place where my turn would come to read and expound the Scriptures. Hence I had been doing my homework on the message to Laodicea.

The Risen Christ accused the Laodiceans of being 'lukewarm' and, in effect, said: 'You make me sick!' This was a reference to the tepid water of Laodicea's medicinal mineral springs which had been channelled down-mountain from Hierapolis, and which were nauseous to the taste. The church at Laodicea had, apparently, fallen for the religion of the Law Party — with its emphasis on externals and religious rites — but were weak on heart religion.

The Risen Christ continued by accusing the Laodiceans of self-satisfaction in their wealth, unaware that, in spiritual terms, they were 'wretched, pitiful, poor, blind and naked'. Situated at the confluence of the Lycus and Meander river valleys, Laodicea represented the gateway to the sea and was one of the richest commercial centres of the ancient world. In AD60 an earthquake laid bare the city. The Roman Empire offered aid towards rebuilding. But the proud city refused all help; no help was needed outside of its own resources . . . .

Having diagnosed the condition, the Risen Christ prescribed the cure. Laodicea — 'the city of gold' — was told to 'buy from me gold refined in the fire'; traditionally taken as a reference to saving faith.

The Risen Christ also told a city noted throughout the Mediterranean world for its black garments made from the black sheep and long-haired black goats that still swarm around the hillsides to buy of Him 'white clothes to wear, so that you can cover your shameful nakedness'. This is taken as a reference to the righteousness of Christ made available by His substitutionary death on Calvary.

Finally, the Risen Christ prescribed 'eye salve'. Laodicea's 'phrygian powder' (eye powder) was the sovereign remedy for ailing eyes throughout the Roman world. The Risen Christ was, apparently, saying, '*You* are the people in need of the eye salve. Buy it from Me. When you have recognized that you have a problem, you will have taken the first step to finding a solution . . . .'

Christianity's oldest heresy, against which Paul made such pointed attacks in his letters, had proved the most enduring. The Law Party that had infiltrated the churches at Antioch and Galatia had preached a sort of spiritual self-reliance, the belief that salvation had to be achieved by human effort. This Christian pharisaism had touched something deep down in the human psyche; an instinct that ran counter to Paul's Gospel of grace.

At the end of the first century, in a city called Laodicea was a Christian church totally satisfied in the efforts it was expending to deserve salvation, unaware that salvation is beyond anyone's deserts, and that, despite its own self-image, it was spiritually bankrupt.

When the Law Party triumphs, Laodicea results.

———

Readings
> Acts 15:1-4, 22-35.
> Galatians 1:6, 7; 2:4; 3:1-11.
> Acts 19.
> Ephesians 2:8, 9.
> Revelation 2:1-7.
> Revelation 3:14-22.

9 FROM PHILADELPHIA TO THE HAGIA SOPHIA

Paul's two to three years in Ephesus included some evangelistic sorties into the surrounding cities. Epaphras, a member of the church at Ephesus but a native of Colossae, was also involved in pioneer evangelism in the region. The Colossian landowner Philemon — whom Paul converted together with his wife Apphia and all his slaves — would doubtless have helped spread the Gospel he had embraced. In one way or another, in the course of the two to three years, 'all the people who lived in the province of Asia, both Jews and Gentiles, heard the word of the Lord.'

Hence, as we visited the seven churches to which John wrote in AD95 we did not feel that the Pauline trail had gone cold. The weather, however, had. And that was to prove a problem.

From Laodicea we set out for Philadelphia (Alasehir). The route was over a mountain range and, before long, the red rock road was covered in snow. Snow filled the sky, first dusting, and then blanketing everything. Capitan's skills as a driver were to be stretched to the limit. Soon after we left the last mountain village behind, and, in second gear, juddered uphill, the road became all but impassable.

During a brief lull in the snowfall, we caught a breathtaking view of snow-covered fields and mountains. We could see over scores of square miles. And we realized that, in all that expanse, we were the only vehicle . . . .

The roads were untreated. When, once more, snow began to billow from the sky, visibility was reduced to a few yards. The road was hazardous in the extreme. With tremendous skill, Capitan managed to turn the vehicle round. Hurtling downmountain rather unnervingly, our driver was also reading a map! He found an alternative route to Philadelphia. It was the one we had taken to Aphrodisias three weeks previously. But, to reach Philadelphia, we had to turn off the main road. The Turkish 'B' road was potholed from the start but, after a few miles, degenerated into a mud-track. Our progress was so slow that a barking dog succeeded in keeping up with us for about half a mile. Eventually, a Turkish car driver travelling in the opposite direction told us that the road was closed ahead. Then, another turn and another direction.

The snow had begun to thin a bit, and came only in large flaky gusts as though someone was opening and shutting a gigantic door. Ahead the snow became smoother; but we passed stranded vehicles partially blocking the main road. After we had travelled through a forested valley heavy with snow, the skies began to clear. As we passed through each township, excited groups of boys snowballed the coach. But we cheered when Capitan found a road to Izmir that went by way of Philadelphia. It was narrow, but took us to our destination.

Philadelphia was the least distinguished and newest of the seven cities. Only a few ruins are visible now. We made the most of what was left of a huge Byzantine church.

The message of the risen Christ to Philadelphia (Revelation 3:7-13) is curious in that it contains no criticism nor condemnation. A garrison city built where the provinces of Mysia, Lydia, and Phrygia met, Philadelphia was a beacon of Greek culture in the first century. 'See,' said the risen Christ, 'I have placed before you an open door that no one can shut . . . .' But, He continued, 'I know that you have little strength . . . .' Philadelphia was a church with a gigantic task to perform, but small numbers. But, if it listened to the Spirit's guidance, mission impossible might be accomplished — and the blessings to be poured out on a triumphant Philadelphia were unparalleled.

Our journey from Philadelphia to **Sardis** was mainly memorable for a long and detailed lecture given by Bilal on the greatness of Kemal Attaturk, the founder of the Turkish nation. Sardis was to prove more interesting. It has the most picturesque setting of all the seven churches. Built on a spur of Mount Tmolus (Boz Dagi) it protrudes from the base of the mountain like the prow of a ship and constitutes a nigh-impregnable citadel.

The Turkish Department of Archaeology has gone to

tremendous trouble in reconstructing the gymnasium at Sardis. Visually, this is most impressive and is labelled in some guide books 'The Palace'. In addition, the site of Sardis contains evocative ruins of the Temple of Artemis and, nearby, the ruins of a Byzantine church.

When John wrote in AD95, the great days for Sardis were already in the past. Although rebuilt after an earthquake in AD17, it had never regained its former glory. The message of the risen Christ (Revelation 3:1-6) makes it clear that what was true of the city was true of the Church. It had failed to live up to early promise and, apart from Laodicea, attracted the most scathing message of the seven. 'I know your deeds; you have a reputation of being alive, but you are dead . . . . Remember, therefore, what you have received and heard; obey it, and repent. But if you do not wake up, I will come like a thief, and you will not know at what time I will come to you . . . .'

The citadel was impregnable; the church was vulnerable in the extreme. It was a socially-distinguished, going-through-the-motions church; it appeared 'worthy' — but appearances were deceptive. Sin had seeped into that church and rotted its body like a cancer.

Nevertheless, writes John Stott in *What Christ Thinks of the Church*, page 83, 'Within that worldly congregation a godly remnant was left. It has always been so. In fact, the doctrine of the remnant figures prominently throughout biblical history . . . .' Even in Sardis there remained 'a little flock' preaching and living Christ's Gospel.

The sun had already set when we left Sardis behind. And so it was under a fresh, clear, morning sky that we made our way to **Thyatira** (Akhisar). To the detriment of archaeological finds, this remains a prosperous Turkish city. The remains of the first century are lost among the modern buildings; and without Bilal we would never have found them. In one place we found, behind barbed wire, the broken columns of a pagan temple. Elsewhere were the inevitable ruins of a Byzantine church. These were being used by children as a playground.

The risen Christ (Revelation 2:18-29) commends the

church at Thyatira for its love, faith, service and perseverance. But in a coded condemnation He continues: 'Nevertheless, I have this against you: You tolerate that woman Jezebel . . . .' This anachronistic reference to an Old Testament pagan queen has puzzled commentators for centuries. The first Jezebel had been a priestess of the Baal cult noted for its sexual excesses. The equivalent in the first-century world was the Greek goddess Aphrodite and the Roman Venus. The cults connected with those goddesses were also associated with gross sexual immorality practised in the name of religion. We can only assume that right in the centre of a church known for its Christian virtue was a cult claiming the prophetic gift, leading the gullible into sexual sin — and being tolerated by the majority. As Paul would write to Timothy (2 Timothy 3:5), it is possible to have 'a form of godliness' but to 'deny the Power' that is the birthright of the second-born Christian. Here, apparently, was the nub of Thyatira's problem.

As we were visiting the seven churches in reverse order, our next destination was **Pergamum**, forty miles distant. It might have been the mood; it might have been the weather — but I found it, apart from Ephesus, the most impressive of the seven sites. What remains of ancient Pergamum is also on a great hill surrounded on three sides by a sprawling modern city, Bergama. On this acropolis are the remains of a most impressive theatre. Thanks to Bilal's taste for the dramatic, he arranged that our first sight of the city should be from the top 'rung' of this unusually steep theatre. As we emerged from the ancient passageway, the scene suddenly broke upon us. The theatre falling away layer upon layer was unnervingly precipitous and, for an instant, we felt that a gust of wind might carry us to our deaths at the bottom of the drop that continued on down beyond the last of the theatre's ruins. It was a heady sensation.

A little cagily, we made our way down from the dizzy heights. To our right we could see the foundations of the ancient temple of Dionysus, the Greek god of wine. And, of course, this 'city set on a hill' had its Byzantine church. To complete this archaeological 'high', nearby were the impressive remains of a temple built to the Roman emperor Trajan and, even more impressive, the excavations of ancient Asklepieon. This had been a Roman centre of healing and the excavations included a complete Roman street as well as a theatre. The Sacred Way, with its columns on either side, was built in honour of the god of healing, Asklepios. There was the medical centre of the ancient world.

Christ's message to Pergamum? (Revelation 2:12-17.) 'I know where you live — where Satan has his throne. Yet you remain true to my name . . . . ' The remainder of the message contains a second reference to Satan's making his habitation in the city, as well as coded allusions to contemporary heresies and heathen practices. The message concludes with a call to repentance.

Why should Pergamum in particular have been considered the habitation of Satan? Our group debated this question. Pergamum had been a centre of pagan religion for centuries. In the first century AD, it would have contained scores of pagan temples and altars. The acropolis then dominated the population centre of Pergamum and was crowned with an immense altar to Zeus. It would have been visible from all points in the city.

Pergamum was also the centre of Caesar worship and had been since permission had been granted to erect a temple 'to the god Augustus'. Behind all pagan worship and the perversions of Christianity represented in code, the risen Christ was saying, was none other than 'the prince of this world'. Hence the Christian's conflict was directly with Satan and his army of malignant spirits from his nightmare dimension. The emphasis of the message to Pergamum: 'God *is* particular, He *is* concerned with right living, and He *is* concerned with truth.'

We had been travelling for a long time. It seemed an age since we had set off from **Smyrna** (Izmir) to follow the footprints of Paul. Hence our return to Izmir and the first sight of the blue-turquoise waters of the Aegean as we descended into the city was a heart-lifting experience.

Of course, because the city has retained its importance down the centuries, it is likely that the ruins of ancient Smyrna are beneath the foundations of Izmir. The agora (market place) of Smyrna, built on the orders of Alexander the Great, has been partially excavated. But if there is anything else, we did not find it.

Christ's message to Smyrna? (Revelation 2:8-11.) 'I know your afflictions and your poverty — yet you are rich! . . . Do not be afraid of what you are about to suffer. . . . Be faithful, even to the point of death, and I will give you a crown of life.'

Roman power and Greek civilization had facilitated the spread of Christianity in the first century. But the corruption at the very heart of Roman government could not but, in the ultimate, have a negative impact on those faithful to the cause of Christ. Both Gaius Suetonius in *The Twelve Caesars* and Cornelius Tacitus in *The Histories* refer to the widespread belief in the early years of Augustus's reign that someone would emerge from Judaea to rule the world. Both Roman historians believed that this prophecy was fulfilled by Vespasian and Titus after the destruction of Jerusalem in AD70. They were, however, aware of the belief among Christians that this prophecy had its origin in the Jewish scriptures and its fulfilment in Jesus Christ.

Anger at the rise of Christianity added to the antisemitism of most of the Roman emperors to create an environment extremely hostile to the movement spreading across the first-century world. The persecution of Christians began, ironically, under the relatively tolerant emperor Claudius. Suetonius writes: 'Because the Jews at Rome caused continuous disturbances at the instigation of Chrestus, he expelled them from the city.'

For many years no fine distinction was made between Jews and Christians, who suffered together. However, we learn from Cornelius Tacitus in *The Annals of Imperial Rome* that the systematic persecution of Christians began with Nero and the Great Fire of AD64 . . . .

The message to the church at Smyrna given in AD95 was to prepare Christians for the greatest onslaught of persecution thus far. It began in the final years of the reign of Domitian . . . .

Following a night's stop-over in Izmir, we made our way through miles of olive orchards to **Troas**, visited by Paul on both his second and third missionary journeys. On the beach, with nothing worse to contend with than a warm wind, we listened to a colleague read from the book of Acts. On his first visit to Troas, Paul had received the vision that led him to cross the sea and begin the evangelization of Europe. On his next visit, he preached a sermon that was so long that a young man sitting on a sill went to sleep and fell out of an upstairs window! That was Paul's farewell sermon prior to his departure for Jerusalem.

For reasons not given, Paul chose to walk alone across the mountains to **Assos**, from where he was picked up by the boat that had sailed from Troas (Acts 20:13, 14). A part of the Roman road he would have taken can still be seen.

However, our coach took a different route to Assos. The road zigzagged for miles over jagged fir-wooded mountains. There were magnificent views of the sea and of valleys. Ten kilometres from Assos the narrow, snaking road brought us to the top of a mountain range affording views of a number of islands. Below we could see a farmer — his plough pulled by two oxen.

The brick road that descended on Assos was almost sheer. None of us will ever forget the sight of sunset over the harbour. Despite a taxing journey, no one was in a hurry to check into the hotel. We all wandered on to the quay from which Paul had taken his departure for Jerusalem, and watched the blood-red sky and water deepen into blackness.

Next morning the coach pulled unwillingly up the same near-to-vertical road surrounded by every dog in Assos bidding a barking farewell. Reaching the top we paused at the third-century church which the Turks had made into a mosque. Our only other stop before we reached Canakkale on the Dardenelles was to examine the site of **Troy**.

Once on the European side of the Dardanelles, we travelled south to see the memorials to the dead of the ill-fated Gallipoli campaign of 1915. From there we took the six-hour journey to Istanbul, arriving in the evening.

This is a city to fire the imagination. Here, in Paul's time, the Egnatian Way began. But, in Constantine's day, Byzantium became the centre of the eastern empire. We were allowed only one day to explore this convenient cross-section of history and culture. We began with the Blue Mosque with its six minarets. With every step we took, it seemed there was someone wanting to sell us something — or polish our shoes! Those with a taste for barter entered the Grand Bazaar with its four thousand shops, and emerged with some genuine bargains.

Thanks to Bilal's insider knowledge — he was a native of Istanbul — we were afforded rapid-fire exposure to all the main sites, on both sides of the Bosphorus, and taken to the best promontories from which it was possible to catch a picture of this imagination-igniting sprawl of a city with its mosques and minarets, palaces and seas, boats and castles, and a history stretching back through Ottoman Turks to Crusaders to Christian emperors to the fall of the Hittite empire in the thirteenth century BC. Since the Bosphorus waterway, the Golden Horn inlet, and the Sea of Marmara became busy thoroughfares for shipping in the fourth millennium before Christ, peoples have passed through the straits from the Aegean and the Mediterranean world to the Black Sea and the barbarous lands of the north.

Byzas, a sailor from Corinth, founded Byzantium in the seventh century BC. Weakened by onslaughts from Roman legions it became a part of the Roman empire in the years immediately BC and, for the century thereafter, enjoyed the benefits of the Pax Romana. Its peace ended when it rebelled against the Emperor Septimus Severus, who in turn besieged, destroyed and rebuilt the city: events commemorated on his triumphal arch in Rome.

Constantine's first exposure to Byzantium was as a conqueror; one of his rivals had made the city a centre of resistance against him. After conquering it in 324, however,

Constantine chose to make it 'the new Rome', a new capital of the Roman empire. It was, in fact, Constantine who pushed back the perimeters of the new city to include the areas around the Golden Horn and the Sea of Marmara, as well as the small city that had formerly straddled the Bosphorus.

Constantine built his palace, the Forum, the Senate, and the first church of St. Sophia by adding to the existing hippodrome on an acropolis. After Constantine's official entrance into his new capital in 330, Christianity and paganism, at first practised side by side, began to meld together into a mix that the apostle Paul would have difficulty recognizing as the religion of Jesus Christ.

When Rome fell to the barbarians in 476, Constantinople became the centre of the civilized world.

We ended our day by entering the building that now stands on the site of Constantine's first church structure: the **Hagia Sophia**. Its interior is far more impressive than its exterior. From the outside it looks like a polyglot of architectural styles reflecting its adaptations over the centuries. It has four minarets dating from its conversion to a mosque after the Turks captured Constantinople in 1453. It includes fortifications and additions that belong to the age of the Latin empire and the crusades. But inside it is possible to get the atmosphere of the Christian church built by Justinian in AD537 (on the site of Constantine's original structure). With its great domes and galleries and ancient mosaics of the Christ, it must have been the most impressive building in the world in the period between the fall of the western empire and the coming of the Turks: a microcosm of the religious history of two continents.

On our last night in Istanbul we looked out at a gorgeous, dusty city with its bubble-domes topped with new moons, its blazing souks, its bursting shops, its incredible flood-lit skyline — and the dark shipping making its way purposefully through the shining waterways. There was a place where east and west met and intermingled and where, behind every stone, lurked some reminder of a distant but remembered past. The city that links two continents also provides the links between two — possibly three — divisions of history: ancient, medieval, modern.

Dawn found us racing for the airport to catch an early flight. Behind us, traffic-laden thoroughfares and brilliant mosques. To the left, shimmering pools of different coloured lights reflected in the busy Bosphorus. On the right, the mean, wooden streets of a seedy city.

It struck me then that what we had had of Istanbul was no more than a flight of impressions like a brilliant surge of tropical fish across a dim aquarium. As we boarded the flight home we wondered what the message of the risen Christ would have been to this boiling of overheated ingredients, the least piquant of which was a micro-minority of Christians . . . .

Readings
Revelation 2:8-3:13.
Acts 15:36-16:10.
Acts 20:7-14.

10 OVER IN MACEDONIA

In high summer AD50, Paul crossed the Aegean from **Alexandrian Troas** to **Neapolis** (Kavalla) in Macedonia. Paul's journey was in response to a vision in which he had seen 'a man of Macedonia' appealing, 'Come over to Macedonia and help us'.

Neapolis was on the **Egnatian Way**, the Roman road that began at Byzantium and continued on to Philippi and Thessalonica. Paul's companions were then three. Silas and Timothy had been joined by Luke at Troas. Luke was a physician who might have come from the ancient world's medical HQ at Asklepeion in nearby Pergamum. To Luke we owe the careful account of Paul's movements in Acts.

Paul's introduction to Macedonia was the beautiful shoreline in which Neapolis nestled; a sight more scenic than ours at Thessalonica's airport. Thessalonica throbs to the same twenty-four-hours-a-day roar and rumble as Athens, but lacks the millennia-old eye-catching artefacts to make it worth the while.

Our exploration of the Pauline places in Greece was in company with a group of exuberant Methodists from two congregations in Wallasey. Having done a last-minute shuffle from Inter-Church to Highway — because of a cancellation — we were taking Hobson's choice and did not know quite what to expect. No sooner had we joined the queue at Gatwick than we were welcomed by the northern-accented ultra-extrovert Revd Peter Hudson, pastor of the Wallasey congregations from which (minus us) the party of fifteen was drawn. In co-operation with Highway, Hudson has been taking his parties of Methodists around the biblical sites of the middle and near East for a quarter of a century. By contrast with Turkey, in Greece the function of Effie, the guide, was to provide instruction only; organization was cared for by the omni-competent Hudson. Annually he works out his own itineraries, costs them carefully, and, I suspect, is never knowingly undersold.

Our trip had got off to a good start. With Eric and Jean, a retired Methodist superintendent and his lady, we were

selected by Olympic Airlines for upgrading to executive class!
Descent on **Thessalonica** was in the dark, the best way to see
it. Our night in a Thessalonica hotel was, beyond question,
the noisiest of our lives. Without air-conditioning and in the
mid-September heat, it was like trying to sleep in a sauna on
the M1. Judging by the number of juggernauts juddering the
streets, I believe this vast industrial city chooses to move its
freight at night to avoid the holiday traffic.

Like all our mornings on 'the Greek trip' we were
'up betimes'; there was something of the puritan in this
Hudson that counted wasted all minutes spent in bed beyond 5 am . . . .

Not that we were sorry to be shot of Thessalonica. As we
left behind its still rumbling streets, there was early-morning
shade on the roads and heat mists partially obscured distant
mountains. Before we were fully awake, Effie was in full flow.
Here was a cemetery dating from the fourth century before
Christ, and here thermal baths used by the ancient — and
modern — Greeks. Travelling east we passed crops of corn,
cotton and tobacco before arriving at two lakes heavy with
fish. The first was dedicated to St. Basil and the name of the
second was Volvis, deriving from Greek mythology. As the
sun burst through and burned off the mist, mountains were
reflected in the calm waters of the lakes.

Beyond the lakes, on the foothills of the mountains, were
stone-built villages. Many of them dated from the exchange
of population between the Greeks and the Turks that
occurred in 1922. The Greeks had moved in from Asia Minor
and the Black Sea area to found new settlements in the nearest part of Greece. They had re-used the names of the villages
from whence they came with the word 'new' in front.

Our route from **Thessalonica** to **Philippi** and **Neapolis**
(Kavalla) followed the Roman Egnatian Way that linked the
Aegean with the Adriatic. We passed through a beautiful
land once given over to blood and battle but now to the
gentle pursuits of agriculture. As we approached ancient
Amphipolis the mountains became more impressive, and
began to enclose. We examined the ruins of a fortified
byzantine city, including four early Christian churches. But

Amphipolis echoes with pre-byzantine memories. The imposing Lion of Amphipolis, excavated after World War II, was sculpted in the fourth century before Christ to commemorate the death of one of the generals of Alexander the Great. This site had been of great strategic importance in Philip the Macedon's policy of uniting the Greek city states against the Persians. At 20, Alexander had inherited his father's conquests and ambition — and expanded both. Crossing to Troas he had defeated the Persians and begun to dream of universal empire. In thirteen years Greece, Asia Minor, Egypt, the Middle East and Northern India had been absorbed, but Alexander never returned home. He had died in Babylon, aged 33, his empire divided among his generals. He had created a mosaic of nations and had built towns and created colonies in which his soldiers had intermarried, co-operating with local rulers. Ironically, it was after the Roman conquest of 168BC that Greek language and culture was successfully enforced on the ancient world.

A *frisson* went through the party as we left the coach at **Philippi**. Renamed after Philip the Macedon in 356BC, the city had become an important centre. It had remained a major centre under the Romans and become the focus of Roman roads, including the Egnatian Way.

Philippi's place in history was ensured when, having sheltered Brutus and Cassius, the assassins of Julius Caesar, for two years, the city was the site of the battle from which Antony and Octavian (Augustus) emerged triumphant. Like Alexander, Octavian was only 20 when he gatecrashed history's front line. But, unlike Alexander, Octavian had a 50-year imperial reign ahead of him.

It is doubtful in the extreme whether anyone, including the immediate participants, viewed the arrival in early August AD50 of an ageing Jew with his mixed bag of companions as being of potentially greater historical significance than the battle of Philippi ninety years earlier. Without question, in Paul's mind he was not crossing from one continent to another. In his day, both sides of the Aegean were culturally Greek and politically Roman. All the little party knew was that, having preached Christ in Cyprus and Galatia, they were about to take His Gospel to Macedonia and Achaia, the provinces of northern and southern Greece respectively. If they had had any fixed plan it would have been to evangelize Macedonia's capital, Thessalonica, and, beyond that, Achaia's capital, Corinth. It is possible that Philippi was evangelized because it was impossible to get to Thessalonica on the Egnatian Way without passing through this city in which, from the absence of a synagogue, it may be assumed that there were fewer than ten male Jews. Philippi was, in fact, a Latin-speaking 'Little Rome', a Roman colony of serving and retired legionaries.

In the absence of his usual springboard for evangelism — the synagogue — Paul and his party went in search of any informal group of Jews and proselytes who might be worshipping outdoors on the Sabbath. They found such a group a mile and a half from the city under the over-arching trees by the narrow Gangites river . . . .

We began exploring Philippi at the spot, by this river, where Paul baptized Lydia of Thyatira. Behind us were blackened fields where the wheat stubble had been burned. Behind that, the modern church of St. Lydia with its beautiful stained glass windows. As a backdrop to the whole scene: the Philippian acropolis.

We walked on to ancient Philippi and examined the three levels of excavation: Greek, Roman, Byzantine. We sat in the agora and walked around the gymnasium. To the south of the site were byzantine ruins. To the north, beyond the modern road, more byzantine ruins but, of greater interest, a cell from the Roman prison . . . .

We paused for a second time to recall the story. We remembered the girl in the grip of the occult forces that seemed so much in evidence in Greece. Our guide reminded us that, later on in the tour, we should be visiting Delphi where the 'oracle' was a magnet for generals and statesmen obsessed with the future and the dark domain of demonic spirits. . . . 'Even as far away as Philippi,' said Effie, 'the power of evil represented by Delphi was very considerable . . . .'

We read how Paul cast the demon out of that youthful

medium and, in doing so, outraged those with a vested interest in the occult. A riot had been the result. Something had snapped, and the populace had gone on the rampage. Ignoring the fact that Paul and Silas were Roman citizens, the authorities had ordered that both be whipped. They had then been half dragged, half carried from the forum across the Egnatian Way into this prison built in the hillside below the acropolis . . . .

Paul had touched a raw nerve in Little Rome. That was, after all, the time when at the imperial centre itself the emperor Claudius was expelling the Jews from Rome because of — in the words of Suetonius — 'continuous disturbances at the instigation of Chrestus'.

We thought how midnight had come in the prison cell cut into the rock below the acropolis; midnight, the hour when occult forces are thought to be dominant. But it found Paul and Silas — who, had they been modern missionaries, might have assumed that God had abandoned them — singing hymns of praise. Their hearts were free before their chains fell off! But earthquakes and tremors were common in Macedonia in the summer. And that quake had been strong enough to throw the stocks loose, dislodge the iron rings that anchored the prisoners' chains, knock the bars off the inner and outer walls and leave them swinging — *and* wake the gaoler.

The next day would see another baptism by the riverside.

When Paul left Little Rome he left the nucleus of a church: Lydia, a textile merchant; the slave girl who was once a medium; and a Roman gaoler.

Isolated in this Latin-speaking city, the Philippian church inherited the storm of persecution that had burst over Paul on his short visit. Writing from prison in Rome in AD63 or 64, in response to a gift the Philippians had sent him, Paul noted that they shared his bonds because they shared his Gospel (Philippians 1:7). But the persecution was all but taken for granted; the real problem that the Philippian letter addressed was that posed by 'those dogs', 'those evil workers' — the Law Party, again!

In the third chapter of this upbeat letter, Paul provided

vital autobiographical details in his argument to prove that, if salvation by works *were* possible, he 'a pharisee of the pharisees' should have achieved it! But, he continued, 'I count all things but loss for the excellency of the knowledge of Christ Jesus my Lord: for whom I have suffered the loss of all things, and do count them but dung, that I may win Christ, and be found in him, not having mine own righteousness, which is of the law, but that which is through the faith of Christ, the righteousness which is of God by faith: that I may know him, and the power of his resurrection, ...' (Philippians 3:7-9, KJV.)

When Paul's party left Philippi they headed west. Our party headed east. We were to spend the night in Neapolis (Kavalla) where Paul had put ashore.

The **Neapolis** Paul knew was destroyed by the Goths. In the fifth century Justinian rebuilt the city and renamed it Christopolis: Christ's city. As we looked out from the balcony of our hotel in this beautiful port, we could see that much remained of byzantine Christopolis. Most evident was a multi-layered Roman aqueduct that dwarfed everything else.

In the evening Effie led the more energetic of our party on a walk around the old town. She showed us the house of Mehemet Ali, the pasha of nineteenth-century Egypt. She showed us St. Paul's church and the capstan where, according to tradition, Paul's boat had been tied up. We watched the sun go down from the castle above the city.

Eleven pm found us in the hotel roof-garden. Both castle and aqueduct were floodlit. From the seaward side we watched the day's last ferry whump its way to Samothrace. The air was cool, the night was deep, furry and dark, while directly below us the street blazed with light . . . .

Next morning, again before we were fully awake, we left behind the fishing boats whose masts protruded through the mists that hovered on the Sea of Thassos. Once the coach had climbed out of the Kavalla basin, we caught sight of a short stretch of the Egnatian Way and imagined Paul and his three friends, stout sticks in hand, setting out on the one-hundred-mile trek to Thessalonica.

Thessalonica was founded by Cassander who named it after his wife Thessalonike, the sister of Alexander the Great. Cicero was exiled there in 58BC and Antony and Octavian repaired there after their victory at Philippi. In the first century AD Thessalonica was the most populous town of Macedonia. In gratitude for its co-operation in the struggle against Cassius and Brutus, Octavian made Thessalonica a free city like Athens. That meant that no Roman soldiers could be stationed there, and that the government was in the hands of an assembly of the people, from whom the magistrates were chosen.

Paul had found no synagogue in Philippi and if, as seems inevitable, he stopped off in Amphipolis, he would have found no synagogue there either. In Thessalonica, however, there was a Jewish community of considerable size and, for three weeks, Paul preached in the synagogue. The central thrust of his preaching would have been to identify Jesus in the messianic passages of the Old Testament. However, from his later letters to the Thessalonians, we find that Paul also preached the glories of the second advent.

Converts were largely among the Gentiles and 'the leading women'. But converts there must have been, and in great numbers. Enough, in fact, to arouse the ire of the Jews who, as in Iconium and Lystra, raised a rabble of idlers. The rabble attacked the house of Jason where Paul was lodging. Failing to find Paul and Silas, the rabble dragged Jason and some other Christians before the magistrate. Because of the expulsion of the Jews from Rome, all Jews and Christians were particularly susceptible to a charge of treason. Later Paul would acknowledge that the Gospel had advanced in Thessalonica in the face of tremendous opposition (1 Thessalonians 1:6 and 2:2).

From Paul's day to our own Thessalonica has been a major sea port. Of the ten million Greek population, four million live in Athens and one million in Thessalonica. Proportionately, its importance was even greater in the Roman period. However, its golden age was the byzantine period when it was the second most important city in the eastern empire after Constantinople.

W. J. Conybeare, writing in 1863, maintained that the church of St. Demetrius in Thessalonica was built on the ruins of the ancient synagogue where Paul had preached. I noted that our guide also took that view, adding, sadly, that the original byzantine church was burned as recently as 1922. However, beneath the church she showed us excavations of Roman baths, and markings that suggested they had been adapted for Christian worship.

H. V. Morton mentioned a tradition that the house of Jason was in the upper town and that the site is now covered by the monastery of Vlattadon. We were shown the site, and, beyond it, visited the acropolis. Somehow, from high above, Thessalonica did not appear nearly as threatening. From this vantage point we also recalled its history. For centuries it had been attacked, unsuccessfully, from the sea. However, the Turks had attacked successfully in 1430 and occupied the city continuously until its liberation in the Balkan wars in 1912.

From this vantage point high above the city we made for Thessalonica's famous museum. The central feature includes exhibits from the royal tombs of Vergina excavated in 1977. The richest items were found in the larger of the two tombs, the one which the excavator believed to have been that of Philip the Macedon. The exhibits include bronze vessels, silver vases, golden coronets, golden jewellery and other articles, the helmet and weapons of the deceased, and a variety of ivory figures. A decorated gold chest from the Great Tomb of Vergina was found to contain bones. From these a complete skeleton has been constructed. The excavator believed it to be the skeleton of Philip the Macedon, the father of Alexander the Great.

For the members of our party of fifteen, a major figure from the late twentieth century AD outshone the major figure from the fourth century BC just before we exited the museum. As we had entered a couple of hours before, we had noticed that security had been particularly stiff. When we came to leave we were told that the last ruler of the now defunct Soviet Union, Mikhail Sergeyevich Gorbachev, was just concluding a lecture he had been giving in another part of the building. We waited for ten minutes and were rewarded by a sight of Gorbachev and his wife Raisa.

A careful reading of Acts 17:1-9 would seem to indicate that Jason and the other Christians were only released by the magistrate on condition that Paul and his immediate companions agreed to leave the city. That he did, going as far as **Beroea** (now Veria), a small town in the foothills of Mount Olympus. Beroea was near enough to Thessalonica to make possible a speedy return to the city should the charges be lifted. Paul might also have been considering another possible course: following the Egnatian Way westward towards the coastal province of Illyricum and, from thence, to Rome. However, Caesar's decree, which had such an impact in faraway Thessalonica, would have made impossible any early plans for visiting Rome.

At first Paul and Silas received a good reception in Beroea. The impact there was in the heart of the Jewish community; there was much earnest examination of scriptural evidence to ascertain the truth or otherwise of Paul's claims about Jesus. Soon Greeks, including once again 'women of high standing', were being drawn towards Christianity. It would appear that Timothy, whom Paul had left behind in Philippi, rejoined him at Beroea. But, following the old pattern, hostile Jews from Thessalonica caught up with Paul and began inciting the crowds. Paul was smuggled to the sea coast. Silas and Timothy remained behind.

As our coach swept southwards, the Olympus range loomed larger and larger. There seemed to be an infinite variety of shades of grey, peak behind peak behind peak. It was easy to see how legends had adhered to those mountains. Those to whom Paul came to preach believed Mount Olympus to be the home of the gods . . . .

Readings
  Acts 16:11-17:15.

11 MOUNT OLYMPUS, THE METEORA AND DELPHI

Litohoro is the last town before gentle foothills become the looming scarps of Mount Olympus. Dominating the town is a deep ravine that goes to the hard heart of the mountain through which a range of peaks is visible, variable distances evident from the endless gradations of grey. A meal under our belts, we were led by Effie on an evening hike five kilometres up the ravine on narrow ledges cut into the rock.

On our return to the town square we looked back to see the sunset light a shelf of cloud against the wall of mountain. The square, we noted, was filled with men — only men — engaged in excited conversation to a background of live music from the tavernas. Whereas the Italians and the Spaniards may have let the afternoon siesta slip, it is observed religiously in Greece. Hence, at the time when the mad dogs and Englishmen who have exposed themselves to the midday sun feel inclined to hit the sack, Greek tavernas and pavement cafes are doing brisk business.

This once, in these unsurpassable surroundings, I joined the natives. Bats swerved and twittered. Above the moan of conversation there was the steady drizzle of the cicadas in the great trees. Green lizards, insatiably curious, came out to watch.

Next morning we bade an unwilling farewell to this place which, in season, is a town of mountaineers. But we had an appointment in Dion. In the words of W. J. Conybeare: 'No city is more likely than Dion to have been the last, as Philippi was the first, through which Paul passed on his journey through the provinces.' From there, or a point near there, the Beroeans saw the apostle off on his sea journey to Athens.

Dion (Greek for Zeus) was a town sacred to the Macedons; a sort of Delphi of the north. No modern settlement is nearby and contemporary archaeologists are lifting an ancient town from the mud in a state of preservation equivalent to that of Ephesus. We walked down completely paved Roman roads, explored an agora surrounded by the plinths of statues and the ruins of temples, shops and — as in Ephesus — a brothel. An unspoiled Roman mosaic of a bull and a Greek mosaic of a town backdropped, like Dion, by Mount Olympus, are there to be admired. The port buildings that might have witnessed Paul's departure have emerged. We watched a female archaeologist at work — temperatures in the upper 90s — with a team of unwilling, coffee-swigging workmen.

From Dion we took the Athens road through what remained of the Plain of Thessaly. Then, at Larissa, the coach struck inland through the ten-mile pass between Mount Olympus and Mount Ossa. That much-fought-over pass is between sheer walls of rock, like the Cheddar Gorge, only a hundred times bigger.

These mountains cut Greece in half. To the north the Plain of Thessaly; to the south a more curious plain that was once a lake. We billeted in Kalambaka, the only town on this second plain.

Dawn out of Kalambaka yielded a scene we shall never forget. We had read up on the **Meteora** but our imaginations could not conjure up something so far beyond previous experience . . . .

At first there was a scarcely discernible stencil-line across what looked like weird monoliths of some unearthly horizon. Then the stencil-line of white became red-orange, growing more livid across the east. The great, monastery-topped rocks appeared, black, incomprehensible, dramatic silhouettes . . . . Then the red-orange became a spectrum of colour, violet covering the rim of the horizon and red-orange rising, the world becoming light, the detail of the monasteries becoming discernible. But the sun itself was still hiding like a promise of eternity behind the Great Meteora.

The Meteora are incredibly tall stone giants rising out of what was once a lake bed. They create one of the world's most spectacular landscapes. Though of differing heights, they all rise hundreds of feet above the level of the plain. They are not mentioned by ancient writers so we may presume that, either they never found them, or that the plain was still waterlogged and the Meteora appeared as islands.

From the eleventh century, hermits began moving into the caves that honeycomb the upper reaches of the rock monoliths. They were followed by monks who built monasteries on the areas of green atop the strange rocks. By the sixteenth century there were twenty-four such monasteries. In the period thereafter, Turkish taxation led to decline and ruin. The Turks also removed the treasures amassed in the monasteries. In the absence of roads and steps, no one visited the Meteora in the earlier centuries. Between 1920 and 1923 steps were cut into the rocks. In the 1960s roads were built.

Only six monastic settlements still function. Supplies are still transported up the sheer face of the rock by nets and baskets. In some cases bridges have been constructed to link monasteries to a nearby mountain wall.

Kalambaka itself is built against a background of these strange rock structures. To visit the only ancient building in the area we climbed halfway up the rock face and entered a beautifully restored byzantine church.

We travelled a few miles by coach from Kalambaka to reach the base of the rock on which the monastery of St. Nicholas is to be found.

It was built in 1523. There, as in the other monasteries, we found valuable libraries containing ancient manuscripts undisturbed, and an equally ancient communal way of life. The monks wore black robes and copes. Every square inch of interior wall space was covered with religious paintings. The painter, Theophanus, was of the Cretan school and, though working in the 1520s, was totally unaffected by Italian Renaissance ideas of perspective and realism. He used dark, primal, earth colours. His painting of Adam's naming the animals, taken on its own, would suggest an innocence of the most fundamental rules governing even medieval art. His representations of heaven and hell in his 'Judgement of the Dead' painting manifest the worst in medieval theology.

But those who undertake the long climb to the monastery of St. Nicholas do so for the views and the novelty of its situation, not for the art of Theophanus.

From the smallest of the monasteries built on the rocky

outcrops, we made for the largest: the Great Meteora. Built in 1382 by St. Athanasius, it was also one of the earliest. Before building the monastery Athanasius had lived in the cave beneath it. In the outer chamber the paintings — again of the Cretan school — represent the various grisly forms of martyrdom suffered by the saints. By contrast, the paintings in the central chamber belong to the Macedonian school of the seventeenth century and revert to biblical themes. This monastery is dedicated to the Transfiguration.

In both monasteries the interior of the dome was dominated by a painting of Christ. I looked in vain for a painting of Paul. Before the end of our visit I was to find a byzantine icon of Paul on Mount Athos. Together with a certificate of authentication I was to buy a hand-painted, wood-mounted copy of this example of traditional byzantine art. On it Paul appears in scholarly mode, with bald head, holding a thick codex.

From Kalambaka we set off on the long, tortuous journey to **Delphi**.

The road snaked over the central mountain range, occasionally affording distant views of scrub-covered uplands, then, beyond, the gently undulating hills where small farmers eked out a living from the thin soil. We passed through mile after mile of forested hills in the slow meander south, turning impossibly sharp hair-pin bends. The roadsides were dotted with home-made shrines that looked like American mailboxes, each commemorating a fatal accident.

The southern mountains were loftier than anything we had seen in the north. Occasionally there would be breathtaking views of deep, dark valleys. And occasionally there would be a glimpse of the shining sea beyond Lamia.

From Lamia on, there were olive trees everywhere. This was, Effie told us, the basis of the main industry of the south. Olives are collected in the same way today as they were in ancient times. In October and November nets are spread on the ground and the olives are shaken from the trees by sticks.

In a high mountain pass before Delphi we encountered a statue of Leonides, a Spartan hero in a decisive victory of

Greek city states over Persians — in 480BC! as with the Greeks on Cyprus, we were finding that mainland Greeks cherished the memories of the personnel of their distant past as if they were heroes of a conflict recently won.

It has been suggested that Corinthian Christians, at some stage, brought the Gospel to Delphi. Nevertheless, for Paul, what it signified was a dark shadow that overcast even the sunniest days of his missionary conquests. For Paul there was an enemy without, and an enemy within. The enemy within was the Law Party whose infiltrators tried to persuade his converts that salvation had to be deserved, not accepted as a gift of God's grace. The enemy without was twofold; the hostile Jews to whom he was a renegade and a sheep-stealer — and the sinister forces of the occult. All occult connections in the ancient world are traceable to Delphi. If the devil had a headquarters on the surface of the planet, there it was.

Delphi, though 570 metres above sea level, was situated at a crossroads of ancient Greece. The 'oracle' might have dispensed her occult wisdom at Delphi as early as 2,000BC. Legend has it that the oracle was based at Delphi because Apollo chose Delphi for a sanctuary. There is, however, another story that the oracle moved to Delphi because of the discovery of a hole in the ground from which 'vapours arose'. Those were believed to arise from the occult world and, hence, to bring with them occult powers, including the ability to forecast the future.

Delphi's 'firm' history stretches back at least to the fourth century BC. Thereafter we find political and military figures from many parts of the Mediterranean world journeying to this distant place to tap into the forces of the diabolic world — against which Paul so graphically warned the Ephesians — before taking major decisions.

In the world of the first century, Nero visited Delphi in AD67, consulted the oracle — then shipped to Rome some 500 statues from the Temple of Apollo! In AD84 the emperor Domitian visited the oracle, and contributed minor repairs to the Temple of Apollo, immortalizing his contribution by a huge Latin inscription that is now kept in the museum.

In the second century the emperor Hadrian visited Delphi

twice (in 125 and 129), providing funds for the restoration of many of the city's buildings.

More ironically, Constantine the Great attended ceremonies in Delphi (and left with works of art to adorn his new capital Constantinople). Julian the Apostate (AD360–363) attempted to revive the ancient occult practices of Delphi that had by his time begun to go by the board.

The fact that Delphi's stadium was also the home of the Pythian Games ensured that the city was a meeting place for political and military heavyweights over many centuries.

Despite what Delphi signified over such a long period, the fact remains that its situation could scarcely be more beautiful, and that the excavations which were begun by the French School of Archaeology in 1892 could scarcely have brought to light a more complete Greek city. Pilgrims who visit Greece almost invariably count Delphi among the high points of their pilgrimage.

We arrived there after a long, winding, sick-making mountain journey — and were immensely grateful to get out of the coach.

Effie came alive on the site of Delphi, of which she was, as a student of archaeology, justifiably proud.

In the sixth and seventh centuries BC, she explained, the oracle had been consulted before the Greeks had made their journeys and fought their campaigns. The sanctuary had originally been decorated by treasures from many places; but those subsequently had been removed, first by the Persians, then by the Romans.

To those high-born visitors who came to Delphi, the high priestess gave 'the oracles'. Originally there had only been one, and the practice had been that she would deliver the 'oracles' on only one day of the year. By the first century AD, however, three priestesses had been in operation.

A fee had been paid and an animal sacrificed before the oracle was sought. The actual oracle was given in the rear of the sanctuary — where the vapours continued to come out of the ground. According to contemporary accounts, Effie explained, the vapours sent priestesses into a trance. The messages they gave while in that trance were generally cryptic and capable of more than one interpretation. There were priests whose task it was to attempt to interpret the messgaes.

'It is the largest archaeological site and the greatest tourist attraction in Greece,' concluded our guide.

Our exploration of the site began on the Sacred Way. Here were a number of 'treasuries', most notably the treasury of the Athenians which has been completely reconstructed.

Above the sacred way is the Temple of Apollo and, in front of its entrance, an agora built in Roman times for the purpose of supplying pilgrims visiting the sanctuary with offerings for the god. The site of the Temple of Apollo has been cleared and a number of pillars have been reconstructed and placed in their original positions. The altar has also been partly reconstructed and partly excavated.

The site of Delphi is on a steep mountainside. Most visitors, having examined the Temple of Apollo, would climb above it to the impressive theatre. In view of the heat that engulfs the site for much of the year, only the more energetic would climb as high as the Delphic stadium. This was the home of the games. Most of the stone seats on which onlookers sat are still in place. The length of the stadium established the main unit of measurement in the ancient world.

The museum of Delphi should not be missed. It contains many statues and busts of famous figures from the ancient world, an unusual number of which — by the standard of other ancient Greek sites — are intact!

Before re-entering the coach we crossed the road to look at the site of the Temple of Athena, enough of which has been reconstructed to provide a vivid impression of its former glory. 'And Athena,' concluded our guide, 'is the god after whom Athens was named. Tomorrow we go to Athens.'

Readings
Ephesians 6:10-18.

THE ATHENS EXPERIENCE

Paul entered Athens alone.

He had known of this city since childhood. It had been the foremost Greek city-state since the fifth century BC and, under Rome, was the intellectual capital of the empire, the home of a philosophical tradition that had included Socrates, Plato and Aristotle. But Paul's visit was not one he had planned to make. The call had been, 'Come over to Macedonia'; he had not given up on his plan to return to Thessalonica.

It is likely that Paul entered Athens under hot September skies, as we did. He had come by sea and seen the white columns of the Temple of Poseidon on Cape Colonna, and the islands of Aegina and Salamis, before coming ashore at Piraeus. We had come by land past Livadia and Thebes, by way of tunnels through the mountains.

Paul's education at the University of Tarsus had, as his speech on Mars Hill was to demonstrate, prepared him to do battle with the philosophers. What caught him by surprise was the primitive paganism among the pseudo-sophistication.

As we had set off that morning we had picked up a new guide, Agiro. She was weak on history, but strong on mythology and contemporary Greece. On some approaches Athens has the appearance of a Third World city. But Agiro drew our attention to the evidence of church building on every hand. Unfortunately, the brand-new, multi-domed Greek Orthodox churches being thrown up in so many places all appear to have come out of the same mould.

As we grumbled our way through Athens' outskirts, it appeared that every conceivable multi-national had its advertisements on the billboards.

As we approached the centre of Athens, air pollution became visible and almost palpable.

We left the coach in St. Constantine's Street. 'Both Constantine and his mother Helena are revered saints in Greece,' explained Agiro. 'We have many churches named after them. St. George is also a great favourite with us.'

The *plaka* is full of atmosphere. Eating in the *plaka*

proved a surprisingly social as well as gastronomic experience. In the streets off the *plaka* there were flea markets with
some genuine bargains. But we were not in Athens for the
shopping . . . .

While Paul waited for Silas and Timothy to catch up with
him, he began to view Athens like a tourist. As now, the
Athens of Paul's day dined out on its past. Nevertheless, Paul
noted a fascination with new fads and ideas. The Athenians
were great talkers, and, 'What's new?' formed the substance
of most of their talk.

Paul was soon in the agora being an Athenian to the
Athenians. He was more than familiar with the two schools
of philosophy then current in Athens: the Stoics and the
Epicureans. Both schools listened to him with a certain jaded
amusement. Although one might expound ideas, why had
that bald-headed Jew got to be so earnest about everything?
After all, when push came to shove, all ideas were equally
good, equally bad, equally meaningless. Why all the excitement?

But Paul *was* excited.

He became *more* excited as, in tourist fashion, he set out
to 'do' first-century Athens. Having touched base with the
Jews in the synagogue, Paul set out for the acropolis and its
Parthenon.

From the moment he had come ashore at Piraeus, the
statue of Athena that dominated all buildings on the
acropolis had been visible. But as he walked the streets of
Athens and, in particular, as he approached the acropolis,
Paul felt that he was passing through a veritable forest of
pagan idols. A mind educated by the finest scholars of Tarsus
and Jerusalem could not but have appreciated the architectural splendours of Athens, but Paul's spiritual propensities
were totally outraged by the stone gods. His whole religious
background in Judaism and Christianity was affronted. All
his days he had served the one true God, Yahweh; and he
would never forget the day outside Damascus when he had
spoken — *actually spoken* — to the risen Christ. Paul was
provoked, and decided to take on the Athenian philosophers.

Stoics and Epicureans listened to what he had to say

about this Jesus who, having been crucified, was alive again; through whose death and resurrection was the gateway to the eternal world. And, as Paul was outraged by the idolatry of Athens, the philosophers were equally outraged by what they perceived as his primitive notions. There was only one thing for it. That unusually combative Jew-with-the-strange-ideas must expound his philosophy in full before the Court of Areopagus on Mars Hill. Paul rose to the challenge and followed the philosophers to the distinctive rock where the court convened — overshadowed by the grandeur of the acropolis.

For centuries, both before and since Paul, myriads of feet have trodden the rock called Mars Hill. As a result, its surface is as slippery as ice. Nevertheless, every Christian who comes to this site regardless of age, and no matter what indignities have to be suffered on the way, must needs get to the top of that hill! Rubber-soled shoes are a great help.

We climbed Mars Hill. In our mind's eye we saw Paul on the white Stone of Shame defending the Gospel of God. And we saw the 'prosecutor' on his Stone of Pride inviting Paul to advance his 'theories'. We may imagine that Paul was in his element. Never had he preached Christ in such a forum. And how could he be ashamed of this Gospel? Not only were five-hundred-plus witnesses to the death and resurrection of Jesus still living, but the significance of this death and resurrection — the Gospel — was 'the power of God unto salvation to everyone who believes'.

As we read Paul's sermon on Mars Hill (Acts 17:22-31), *we* are impressed: 'Men of Athens! I see that in every way you are very religious. For as I walked around and looked carefully at your objects of worship, I even found an altar with this inscription: TO AN UNKNOWN GOD. Now what you worship as something unknown I am going to proclaim to you . . . .'

And, as Paul unfolded his Gospel, he interwove a reference that reflected Plato's *Republic* (the tenth book). He managed to echo a passage of the *Eumenides* of Aeschylus in which Athene tells how this Court on Mars Hill came to be set up. Then he cross-referred to Plato again, who had

written of the great Architect of the Universe. Paul spoke of
One who 'himself gives all men life and breath and everything else . . . '. He managed to interject direct quotes from
the Cretan poet Epimenides and the Silesian poet Aratus.
Then there was a throw-away line from Euripedes.

But there was a problem. We cannot hear the tone of
Paul's voice. We can, however, imagine it. From the structure
of his sermon it is clear that he regarded Greek poets and
philosophers as representing no more than the pastel shades
of wisdom, by comparison with the vivid primal colours of
the God who was, in Christ, reconciling the world unto Himself. He concluded on the high note of the resurrection of
Jesus.

But his reception on Mars Hill was one of sneering and
suppressed laughter. The 'prosecutor' from the Stone of
Pride told him with barely concealed arrogance that he must
come again sometime. But there was at least one man
present, Dionysius, after whom the Roman Catholics have
dedicated their cathedral in Athens, who followed Paul down
the slopes of Mars Hill. He wanted to hear more, and right
away. He couldn't wait. Elsewhere in Athens there were 'a
number of others', including 'a woman named Damaris', who
were influenced by Paul's words. But in Athens there were no
conversions, no baptisms.

The court of Areopagus had, in effect, denied Paul
licence to teach. But we cannot imagine that Paul remained
silent . . . .

From Mars Hill we climbed the acropolis and were treated
to a detailed history of all its many ancient structures. The
twelve-metre statue of Athena, covered in gold and ivory, that
would have dazzled the eye of Paul was, in common with
many Greek treasures, removed to Constantinople (and there
destroyed in one of that city's many conflagrations). There
are four main monuments to be seen on the acropolis:

- The Parthenon, completed in 438BC, built in the Doric
  style and dedicated to Athena.
- The Propylaea, through which we climbed the steps to
  enter the acropolis, built immediately after the Parthenon
  — but never completed!

- The Temple of Athenamiki, also known as The Temple of the Winged Victory, massively impressive, and built of Ionic columns to commemorate the victory of the Greeks over the Persians in 479BC.
- The Erechtheion, with the Porch of the Caryatids, completed circa 394BC (though the present caryatids are copies, the originals being divided between the Acropolis Museum and the British Museum).

Looking immediately down from the acropolis is the theatre of Dionysos, the oldest of the Greek theatres, dating from the fourth century BC; and the theatre of Herod Atticus, a restored Roman theatre that is still in use.

As I left the acropolis to go in search of the coach, I noted something I had missed before: the complete text of Paul's sermon on Mars Hill set into the side of the hill. Someone was reading it out to a 'congregation' of approximately two hundred.

Then it struck me. While it is hard to imagine Paul's firing on any fewer than six cylinders, had there been any inclination on his part to do so as he left Athens behind, if he had felt any residual embarrassment with regard to his speech to the philosophers, it would have disappeared had he been able to see the future. His Mars Hill speech has gone down to posterity along with the Funeral Oration of Pericles and the Philippics of Demosthenes as one of the great speeches of Athens. Today there is no sign of the Stoics or the Epicureans but, nearly 2,000 years on, the Greek national flag is lowered to half mast on each anniversary of the crucifixion they despised, and raised to commemorate the day of resurrection that caused them to snigger.

From Athens we headed south for **Nafplio**. Nafplio had, said our guide, been mentioned by Homer, circa 800BC, as an important kingdom at the time of the Trojan War, but had gone into decline thereafter. In fact, over the next five days of our residence there, we were to find it a most fascinating centre. With its Crusader castle and Venetian hilltop fortifications, there is something ethereal about this small resort that the Greeks chose as their capital in 1821 after they had won their freedom from the Turks. Bathed in the insouciance of drowsy days, we were to spend contented hours in the dappled sunlight of its canopied quayside cafes. And from Drepano each evening we watched the sun go down into a violet sea.

———

Readings
> Acts 17:16-34.
> 1 Corinthians 15:1-22.

Miletus, where Paul presented his farewell message to the Ephesian elders. These are the ruins of a typical Greek theatre.

Pergamum had a spectacular theatre. It looks down on the modern town. Pergamum was a centre for the cults of Zeus, Athena and Dionysus.

Sardis, and the gymnasium renovated from the Hellenistic period. Nearby are the ruins of the Temple of Artemis.

Hierapolis was built on a mountainside of calcified rock. It has hot mineral springs from which the water flows down to Laodicea.

The Great Theatre of Ephesus, and the road that once led to the harbour. During Paul's visit this was the scene of a riot.

Ephesus is the greatest archaeological site of all. This mosaic pavement is off Curetes Street.

There is little to be seen of the Temple to Artemis, the pride of ancient Ephesus. These are the ruins of a Temple to Hadrian, the Roman Emperor.

Almost certainly, the site of Paul's shipwreck on Malta.

ANNO M DCCCC XIII
US ET VICESIMUS NATIONUM
AR CONVENTUS DE MYSTER
S ET SANGUINIS IESU CHRIS
EMPLO TAMQUAM PRINCIPE
UA EXCEPTUS EST AD DIES
AS VIII VIII VII KAL MAIAS HORA
NA LECATUS PONTIFICIS MAXIMI
JAPURATUS ET CONLEGAE BINI
RA CORAM CONSEDERUNT IUXTA
UM MEDII ALTARIS GRADUM
UNT ARCHIEPISCOP QUINDECIM
PI QUINQUE ET QUADRACINTA
ES MULTI KLERUS UTRIUSQUE
PLURIMUS DEINDE PROCERES
MATES EXTERI PATRICIQUE ET
S NOSTRI EPHEMERIDUMQUE
RES POSTREMO MAGNA CIVIUM
E OFFICIIS PACISQ FREQUENTIA
QUE INFERIOR AREA QUIDQUAM
T LITTERIS PONTIFICIIS PRIMO
ESSU RECITATIS AUGURALIQUE
IONE A LEGATO HABITA SACR
RES INGENIO ET ELOQUENTIA
ORBE INSIGNES PRAETERE
ORES VIRI PROFAN AT PII ET
IONE PRAESTANTES ARGUME
INO MYSTERIO VARIA
NIS ET OBERRA AUD

MARCANO

JOSEPH GRECH
DONAVIT MCMLXXIV

S: PAVLVS

A statue of the Apostle Paul outside the massively domed church in Mosta, on Malta.

The Church of St. Paul in the 'Silent City' of Mdina, Malta. Mdina was built over the site of the Roman capital on the island, Melita.

The view to the probable site of Paul's shipwreck from the walls of Mdina.

The exterior of Rome's Colosseum where many of those who embraced Paul's Gospel were to perish.

The interior of the Colosseum.

The Vatican, across the Tiber. Paul was executed in Rome during the reign of Nero.

13   CORINTH AND THE SOUTH

Not that our six days in the Peloponnese were spent in idleness. There was, if memory serves, only one rest day. But the programme was not quite as 'packed' as in the pre-Athens period. We were permitted space to take in the atmosphere.

We spent one complete day, on which the sun burned like a brazier, travelling to and from Olympia. On the map the Peloponnese did not look far from one side to the other. But it is chock-full, coast to coast, with mountains. And big ones at that. Snake passes link one town to the next; roads are steep, precipices sheer, hair-pin bends sharp, and everything depends on the skill of the coach driver, and the brakes . . . .

We lost count of the vicious hair-pin bends through the mountains between Nafplio and Tripolis but we were grateful that, for some miles, a new road had been carved through the rock; going through made a nice change from zigzagging around the mountain.

Somewhere beyond Tripolis was a tiny region-within-the-region infested with cherry orchards. From time to time we would pass mule-mounted peasants. Then there would be a line of donkeys tethered together, trotting along a path by the roadside with panniers full, raising, among them, a plume of dense dust.

On the long journey to Olympia we had plenty of opportunity to observe the flora as well as the fauna. Lines of Judas trees that blossom at Easter were pointed out to us, as were the white and pink of the Oleander, and the orange Pyracantha.

At a point when we had given up on ever arriving at Olympia, Agiro announced, 'No point in Greece is more than fifty kilometres from the sea.' Not long afterwards we caught sight of the Ionian Sea with its deep blue waters set with islands and contrasting with the pale, lime-green forestry of the shoreline.

After a five-hour drive we arrived at **Olympia** where, circa a thousand BC, the games began. *Organized* games, according to Agiro, commenced in 776BC. That was the age of the Greek city states. The games continued into the Macedon period, were discontinued in the Roman period, and not recommenced until 1896. The ceremony of the torch and 'the eternal flame' began as recently as the Berlin Olympics of 1936. In an Olympic year the flame is carried from the site of ancient Olympia, first to Athens, and from there to the city selected for the games.

The site of Olympia is large and contains some interesting excavations. We examined a byzantine church. Central to the site are the ruins of the temple of Zeus. Among the other features are the ruins of the temple of Hera. What captures the imagination, however, is the tunnel — still in place — through which contestants ran or rode to participate in events in the stadium. We sat on the spectators' benches as Peter Hudson read, 'Know ye not that they which run in a race run all, but one receiveth the prize? So run, that ye may obtain . . . .' (1 Corinthians 9:24, KJV.)

The metaphor of games and competition was certainly employed in Paul's writings more than once, lending credance to the tradition that he preached in Olympia. Making a point against the perfectionists who were influencing the Philippian church, Paul wrote; 'Not that I have already obtained all this, or have already been made perfect, but I press on to take hold of that for which Christ Jesus took hold of me. Brothers, I do not consider myself yet to have taken hold of it. But one thing I do: Forgetting what is behind and straining towards what is ahead, I press on towards the goal to win the prize for which God has called me heavenwards in Christ Jesus . . . .' (Philippians 3:12-14.) Under the sun's noon glare and the parching heat, the sky over Olympia seemed to weigh a ton.

Days began to melt and fuse together in the heat of late September.

There were boat trips out of Nafplio.

There was a visit to an orthodox service; and impressions of cantors, spade-bearded priests with their incantations — and a poor woman withdrawing from the service in tears and hiding in the shadows, feeling unworthy to participate.

There was the visit to the fourth-century-BC theatre at **Epidavrus** in the coolth of an early morning when the tang of autumn was beginning to scent the air. There were visits to Mycenaen castles and fortified cities that Agiro told us predated Moses by two thousand years. One was at **Tiryns**. And there was the acropolis of **Mycenae** itself . . . the Lion Gate, the paved streets. . . . A mountain fort believed to have been the palace of Agamemnon, where he is said to have been murdered by his wife and her lover on his return from the Trojan Wars (c 1,200BC) . . . the walk down one hundred or more steps to a water cistern reminiscent of old Jerusalem . . . the beehive tomb like a pyramid with its imposing entrance topped by a hundred-and-twenty-ton stone . . . .

A stopover at **Patras**, where legend has it that Andrew was crucified on an X-shaped cross in AD68 . . . and the connected legend of a byzantine naval officer given the task of carrying the remains of the apostle to the end of the world and, in the event, putting ashore in Scotland; though the cathedral at Patras, overlooking the Gulf of Corinth, still claims some of Andrew's remains . . . .

The trip by rack-and-pinion railway through the Vouraikos Gorge . . . and the unscheduled journey to the monastery at Mega Spileo which prizes an icon believed to have been painted by St. Luke . . . .

The unforgettable visit to Kalavrita where, on 13 December 1943, the entire male population was massacred by the Nazis . . . a cross and a sculpture, the latter containing the names and ages (some as young as 14) of those slaughtered . . . the school building where the women and children were herded to be burned to death . . . in Greek the chalk-stone words: NO MORE WAR.

Kastria and a complex of underground caves; a 'cathedral' with stalactites and stalagmites, plus strange formations of calcium and limestone . . . used in World War II by the Resistance . . . .

But I was impatient to visit Corinth. *So* impatient that I was up and active well before dawn on the day the visit was scheduled . . . .

Darkness clung to the vineyards and olive groves of Drepano. A faint, pale-green light over an eastern mountain ridge was the first suggestion that light and warmth might yet return to the world. Gradually, indistinct trees became distinct and cast long shadows towards the west . . . .

The pale yellowish-green fused and burned and became orange. Then, suddenly, the fireball appeared from behind a distant peak. The day was born. Every mountain took on its own shade of grey according to its distance and the angle of the sun.

Then, in minutes, the fireball rose in the sky in triumph, intensifying light and shadow, streaking the landscape. Only among the oleander in the deepest recesses of the valleys did darkness reign on. And in the ramshackle that housed the poor, there its reign would continue to sadden noon and hasten nightfall.

But our world was up and awake. Everyone cried, 'Kalimera!' to everyone else as if morning had never happened before, and their dearest wish had been to rise from slumber and draw strength from its warmth.

Before the sun gained much in strength, we had set off through Nafplio, the Venetian castle atop the hill looking like the Great Wall of China.

Passing through villages on the way to **Corinth** we saw schoolchildren herding into buildings to learn history from books. But history was all about them and above them, from the crumbling Mycaen stones to Greek theatres and gymnasia, and Roman roads.

On our way from Athens five or six days before, we had our first look at the amazing Corinthian Canal. Now we looked again and learned something of its history.

The isthmus of Corinth had always been the only bridge connecting mainland Greece to the Peloponnese. Corinth had been built because of the advantages to be gained from settling near this natural bridge. There were benefits to be had from controlling the passage across the isthmus. At the same time, the settlement could found its economy on the exploitation of the two seas on either side of the isthmus and on trade relations with all points east and west.

Homer refers to Corinth as a minor provincial centre, politically dependent upon the kingdom of Agamemnon. But as trade grew Corinth grew; and the Corinthians began to speculate on the advantage to be gained from creating a passage through the isthmus. Long before the Christian era, Periander developed a plan to cut a canal through the isthmus. Some time later Demetrios Poliorketes laid out an even more elaborate plan. Further studies were undertaken by Julius Caesar, Caligula and Hadrian. Caligula even sent men to the isthmus of Corinth in AD40, actually to make plans to implement one of the schemes. No work began because it was discovered that the sea level of the Corinthian Gulf was higher than that of the Saronic Gulf.

In AD67 Nero sent several thousand workmen to begin to dig their way through the isthmus of Corinth. Digging began at either end and the plan was for the workmen to meet in the middle. Nero's death put an end to the project and it was not resumed until 1881. The Corinth Canal was completed in 1893. It is sixty kilometres long, twenty-one metres wide, and the water is eight metres deep. It is fascinating to watch whole lines of ships pass through.

But canal or no canal, Corinth's importance in the first-century world and its trade links with all points of the compass made it a strategic location for the spread of the Gospel. According to Philo, there were Jewish communities 'in most of the best parts of the Peloponnese'. However, the largest Jewish community was in Corinth. It is estimated that, following the expulsion of the Jews from Rome by Claudius 'because of Chrestos' in AD49, the Jewish community swelled to twenty thousand. Among the Jews who came from Rome to settle in Corinth were Aquila and his wife Priscilla. They had already embraced the cause of Christ and, like Paul, were by trade tentmakers (Acts 18:1-3).

We do not know whether Paul travelled by land or sea from Athens to Corinth. Either way, he was afforded time to plan his strategy. It is possible that he thought there were lessons to be learned from the Mars Hill experience. At all events, some years later, when he recalled his first arrival in Corinth, he wrote; 'When I came to you, brothers, I did not come with eloquence or superior wisdom as I proclaimed to you the testimony about God. For I resolved to know nothing while I was with you except Jesus Christ and him crucified.

I came to you in weakness and fear, and with much trembling. My message and my preaching were not with wise and persuasive words, but with a demonstration of the Spirit's power, so that your faith might not rest on men's wisdom, but on God's power.' (1 Corinthians 2:1-5.)

It was natural that Paul took lodgings with Aquila and Priscilla and that the first Sabbath found him reasoning in the synagogue, 'trying to persuade Jews and Greeks' about the Gospel of Jesus Christ.

Now that Silas and Timothy, doubtless having taken the land route, had arrived from Macedonia, Paul was able to devote himself 'exclusively to preaching'. When, according to previous pattern, the Jews became abusive, Paul made it clear that he had done his duty in presenting the Gospel to them first; '"I am clear of my responsibility. From now on I will go to the Gentiles."' (Acts 18:6.)

Paul didn't move far. The house next to the synagogue was owned by Titius Justus 'a worshipper of God'. Paul continued his preaching there. His first converts were, perhaps, surprising ones; 'Crispus, the synagogue ruler, and his entire household believed in the Lord; and many of the Corinthians who heard him believed and were baptized.' (Verses 7 and 8.)

Modern Corinth is miles away from ancient Corinth. Hence enough of the Corinth Paul knew remains to evoke its atmosphere. The site of Corinth is more evocative of the Pauline story than any other in Greece.

South of the city's agora the skyline is still dominated by the volcano-shaped Acrocorinth. Nineteen hundred feet high, it dominated the city and on a clear day was visible from Athens. On that acropolis was the temple of Aphrodite or Venus, goddess of love. Paul had encountered a similar cult in Antioch and on Cyprus. It was a cult in which sexual promiscuity was practised in the name of religion. A thousand female slaves or priestesses served the temple of Aphrodite by roaming the streets of Corinth and practising prostitution.

Dean Farrar called Corinth 'the Vanity Fair of the Roman Empire'. William Barclay wrote; 'the very name Corinth was synonymous with debauchery. . . . There was one source of evil in Corinth which was known all over the civilized world. Above the isthmus there towered the hill of the acropolis . . . .' John Stott says; 'the sexual promiscuity of Corinth was proverbial, so that *korinthiazomai* meant to practise immorality, and *korinthiastes* was a synonym for a harlot.' John Pollock writes; 'If the love of Christ Jesus could take root in Corinth, the most populated, wealthy, commercial-minded and sex-obsessed city of Eastern Europe, it must prove powerful anywhere.'

And it *did* take root. The power of the Gospel was proof against hedonism in its most extreme form as well as the materialism of the commercial capital of the Roman empire. But, as Paul well knew, though the 'old man of sin' was legally dead when an individual was 'born again', 'the old man' didn't know it — and kept rapping on the coffin lid! The sins of the past resurfaced and had to be addressed by Paul in his letters to Corinth. 'The body is not meant for sexual immorality,' insisted Paul when he wrote from Ephesus in AD55, 'but for the Lord, and the Lord for the body. By his power God raised the Lord from the dead, and he will raise us also. . . . Flee from sexual immorality . . . .' (1 Corinthians 6:13-18.)

But in the midst of it all, the Gospel had its triumphs. Paul listed the sins for which Corinth was infamous: sexual immorality, idolatry, adultery, male and female prostitution, homosexuality, thieving, greed, drunkenness, slander, swindling. Then, when he had finished his list, he added with triumph in his tone: 'And that is what some of you were. But you were washed, you were sanctified, you were justified in the name of the Lord Jesus Christ and by the Spirit of our God.' (1 Corinthians 6:9-11.)

But the trembling and trepidation with which Paul had approached this city of a quarter of a million souls was not without good reason. It is clear that Paul's life was in danger, either from conspiring Jews or from the debauched mob in this port-metropolis, or from both. At all events, the risen Christ appeared to Paul with a message to infuse him with no-matter-what courage: 'Do not be afraid; keep on speaking, do not be silent. For I am with you, and no one is going to attack and harm you, because I have many people in this city.'

Commissioned thus, Paul remained in that sink of iniquity and preached his Gospel fearlessly for one-and-a-half years. The crisis, when it came, came from the Jews. But, in keeping with the promise of Christ, they were unable to harm Paul. They took him to court 'while Gallio was pro-consul of Achaia'. And Gallio, proconsul in AD51–52, was the younger brother of the Stoic philosopher Seneca, tutor of the youthful Nero. Seneca made it a matter of record that his brother was totally committed to justice and tolerance. That, certainly, was Paul's experience of him. When Paul appeared before Gallio in the forum, Gallio listened to the charges, then demolished them, ruling that there had been no misde-meanour or crime — then he ejected the Jews from the court. Humiliated, and angry because of the failure of their well-laid conspiracy, the Jews 'all turned on Sosthenes the synagogue ruler and beat him in front of the court. But Gallio showed no concern whatever.' (Acts 18:17.)

Tradition, backed by the judgement of some archaeol-ogists, has identified the site where Paul was brought before Gallio with the *bema*. Like the *rostra* in the forum in Rome, the tribune in Corinth, called in Greek a *bema*, faced the agora and was flanked by central shops on either side. That *bema* was used by officials for appearances before the public and for judicial hearings. In Paul's time the *bema* was cer-tainly an impressive structure.

Meanwhile, Paul continued to preach Christ everywhere. Christ was being gossiped in the gymnasia, in the theatres, in the baths and the houses of the merchants, and in the many streets. A surprising number of those places remain in this great city where, against all the odds, the cross scored a major triumph.

But Paul would always have to display a great deal of patience with those who embraced the cause of Christ in Corinth. The Corinthians, it would appear, were slow to mature in their Christian experience. The promiscuity they had learned from the cult of Aphrodite would recur, as would the homosexuality they had practised at the temple of

Apollo. The Corinthian church would appear to have been given to over-excitement; Paul had much to teach them in his letters about the gifts of the Spirit, and how 'tongues' were so easily counterfeited. But Paul had love in his heart for the Corinthians. He continued to introduce them to 'the more excellent way' . . . .

There were times in Paul's letters when his detailed, scholarly argumentation was left behind; and when his clinical, theological explanations were abandoned. On those occasions his words simply soared into the realms of prose-poetry. Having instructed the Corinthians on the pitfalls of 'tongues', he soared into the finest panegyric on love ever committed to paper: 'If I speak in the tongues of men and of angels, but have not love, I am only a resounding gong or a clanging cymbal. . . . Love is patient, love is kind. It does not envy, it does not boast, it is not proud. . . . Love does not delight in evil but rejoices in the truth. . . . Love never fails. But where there are prophecies, they will cease; where there are tongues, they will be stilled; where there is knowledge, it will pass away. For we know in part and we prophesy in part, but when perfection comes, the imperfect disappears. . . . Now we see but a poor reflection as in a mirror; then we shall see face to face. Now I know in part; then I shall know fully, even as I am fully known. And now these three remain: faith, hope and love. But the greatest of these is love.' (1 Corinthians 13.)

What a message for the city where love had been devalued and debased! When they heard it, the Corinthians would see again the ageing Jew with fire in his belly, standing in the dock at the *bema*, his back to the symbol of evil, holding forth on the principles of truth.

Readings

Acts 18:1-18.
1 Corinthians 2:1-5.
1 Corinthians 6:9-11.

14   SEA JOURNEY, CAESAREA
         AND JERUSALEM

In the museum of Corinth we used time exposure to photograph the two massive figures that once stood on either side of the entrance to ancient Corinth. It must have been with a heavy heart that Paul passed these great monoliths on his way to take ship from **Cenchreae**. He had entered Corinth with great trepidation but was leaving it in the knowledge that the city that posed the greatest challenges had afforded the greatest rewards.

We followed him to his port of embarkation, Cenchreae. There Paul was overwhelmed with gratitude to God and, as with any Jew who was thanking God for some blessing or some deliverance, he took a vow. Then, with Aquila and Priscilla, he sailed to Ephesus, his first visit to that city. There Aquila and Priscilla remained, but, after a brief consultation in the synagogue, Paul sailed on to Caesarea and travelled from there to his home base at Antioch.

From the air the two arms of Cenchreae's ancient harbour can be seen through the translucent waters of the Aegean. A section of the south quay is still above low tide. Pillars from Roman Cenchreae are jumbled with the ruins of a byzantine church in this city that was once the eastern port of Corinth. In the second century AD Lucius Apuleius described Cenchreae as 'a mighty haven frequented with the ships of many nations'.

Paul's triumph in Corinth gave him the confidence to take on the other two great cities of the ancient world, Ephesus and Rome. Thus, after a short summer, during which he might have travelled from Antioch to Jerusalem, he set out on his third missionary journey in August 52. On the landward route to Ephesus he visited for the fourth time the southern Galatian churches of Derbe, Lystra, Iconium and Pisidian Antioch. But Ephesus was always his goal. There he remained for between two and three years.

From **Ephesus** Paul sent disciples into the surrounding area. That, almost certainly, was what he had done from

Corinth since there is a persistent tradition that Corinthian Christians went out as far north as Delphi and, to the south, throughout the Peloponnese during and immediately after Paul's stay in the city.

But Paul could never forget Macedonia and, more especially, the fact that he had unfinished business in the port city of Thessalonica. From Macedonia he travelled briefly southward, but once more became the victim of jealous Jews.

A U-turn took him back to Macedonia and into a tortuous itinerary in the course of which he visited both Troas and Philippi. F. F. Bruce believed that, 'at some point during this period, Paul appears to have traversed Macedonia from east to west along the Egnatian Way and turned north into Illyricum'. Paul told the Romans (15:19) that he had 'fully proclaimed the gospel of Christ' in **Illyricum**, the mountainous land that borders on the Adriatic.

Concluding this third missionary journey, he joined the ship at **Assos**, calling briefly at **Miletus** to address the Ephesian elders. There are hints in his message that he had the end of the road in view; '"I am going to Jerusalem, not knowing what will happen to me there. I only know that in every city the Holy Spirit warns me that prison and hardships are facing me. However, I consider my life worth nothing to me, if only I may finish the race and complete the task the Lord Jesus has given me — the task of testifying to the gospel of God's grace."' (Acts 20:22-24.)

From hints given in the epistles it is clear that Paul had suffered 'great affliction in Asia' already, that was not detailed in Acts. The Ephesus years produced a number of letters, some of which might have been completed in the period immediately thereafter. In early AD55, Asia was governed by those who had murdered Silanus and records in Rome contain details of their tyranny. Paul's second letter to Corinth was written 'out of great distress and anguish of heart' (2:4); and though 'the eternal weight of glory' outshone all persecutions, persecutions were 'sore' while they lasted; and what he was suffering then, the Corinthians could expect to suffer before long (4:17; 6:3-13; 8:2). In the great testament of faith he wrote from Ephesus to the Roman church, there may also be a hint that in Ephesus occult powers were turned on him (Romans 8:38, 39). But if Paul was afflicted, he was not 'struck down'. The Gospel had yet to be taken to many lands including Spain. Paul also had a burning desire to speak in person to the Roman Christians to whom he had sent his greatest letter.

Meanwhile, in April AD57, his pressing project was to take the proceeds of the great collection to the impoverished church in Jerusalem.

From Miletus he 'sailed straight to Cos', an island immediately due south of Miletus. **Cos** was famous for its temple of Asklepios. As they lay at anchor, Paul's chronicler, Dr. Luke, would have reflected that that was the city of Hippocrates.

Next day they sailed past Cape Triopium and the peninsula of Cnidus to land at the capital of the island of **Rhodes**. There Paul would have seen the remains of the Colossus, one of the seven wonders of the ancient world; an impressive bronze monument built between 304 and 284BC, but chiefly destroyed in an earthquake in 225BC. In Rhodes it is believed that Paul preached on their island and appointed Procorus, one of the seven deacons (Acts 6:5) as their bishop. 'St. Paul's harbour' on Rhodes is situated at the foot of the acropolis of Lindos; this is in line with another local tradition that maintains that Paul used the opportunity to challenge the worship of Athena Lindia which, for centuries, had been practised on the island. Much continues to be made of Pauline tradition on Rhodes; there is a St. Paul's Gate and even a belief that one of the Pauline letters was written to the islanders . . . .

From Rhodes they sailed due east to **Patara**. There they 'found a ship crossing over to Phoenicia' and boarded it. From there they sailed to **Tyre**, sighting Cyprus on the way. After a seven-day stop-over with Christians in Tyre, during which the ship was doubtless reloaded, the vessel took them on to **Ptolemais** (Acre), twenty-five miles south. Once again there was a party of Christians to greet them and afford them hospitality. Next day they left, finally putting in at **Caesarea**.

Just enough remains of Roman Caesarea to make it worth

a visit for the modern Christian. The Tel Aviv to Haifa motorway hugs the coast and hence passes very close to the site of Caesarea. It is a curious motorway; there are donkeys, the occasional camel, and frequent vendors of fruit occupying the slow lane!

What is left of Caesarea is strung out along one-and-a-half miles of coastline. Of great interest is a dedication stone from the Roman theatre which bears the only extant inscription naming Pontius Pilate. Pilate, in common with other procurators, lived at Caesarea, the first-century capital of Palestine.

The Roman theatre from which the dedication stone has been taken has been rebuilt by the Israeli Department of Antiquities. Facing out over the Mediterranean, it is still in use for concerts and occasional religious gatherings. Also of interest on the site are the remains of a Crusader fortress.

There is very little to show for the massive investment that Herod the Great poured into building this city between 25 and 13BC. At the turn of the eras, Caesarea was a showpiece capital, a completely new city with a modern harbour. Herod's engineers had made use of the very latest concepts. They had constructed a number of piers for the berthing of ships, together with storage buildings and hostels for seamen. There, as elsewhere, Herod left evidence of his cynical attitude towards religion; under his instruction a number of temples to Caesar Augustus were constructed. The entrance to the harbour was flanked by huge statues. The city was well planned with markets, public baths and — almost all that remains — the theatre. A large section of a Roman aqueduct, dating from shortly after Herod's time, separates the beach from the sand-dunes just north of the site.

What caught Paul's eye among the marble public buildings as he put ashore at Caesarea was, almost certainly, Herod's palace. Before long, that would play a major part in his story. On this occasion, however, he made for the house of Philip the evangelist. There considerable pressure was placed on Paul not to make his planned journey to Jerusalem.

When he set off for Jerusalem, Paul was accompanied by

a group of Caesarean Christians. In **Jerusalem** he lodged with Mnason, one of his converts from Cyprus. By contrast with the frigid reception he had received when he had first visited Jerusalem as a Christian, Paul was now accorded the warmest possible welcome. Luke heard him recall, in detail, the triumphs of the Gospel in the lands of the Gentiles. While rejoicing, the Jerusalem Christians expressed concern at how the Law Party would receive the news of so many Gentile converts. Evidently, the Jerusalem Council notwithstanding, the Law Party continued to teach that man was not saved by Christ alone, but by Christ plus law keeping. Paul had no quarrel with the law but was always at pains to emphasize that obedience was the fruit, not the root, of salvation.

Seeing him in the temple to fulfil the vow he had made while in Cenchreae, the Jews turned on him ostensibly because he had introduced a Gentile from Ephesus into the temple area. The riot spread from the temple area to the city at large; 'The whole city was aroused, and the people came running from all directions'. (Acts 21:30.) Paul was dragged bodily from the temple, and the gate slammed shut behind him.

The Jews had been against Paul from the first, but the amazing thing about the detailed account provided by Luke is that it contains not the slightest hint of anti-semitism. The picture comes across that the Jews were wrong-headedly determined to misunderstand Paul as they had misunderstood Jesus and Stephen before him. But the charge against Paul was a significant one. The allegation against him was that he had taken a Gentile beyond the outer court (the Court of the Gentiles) of the temple, beyond the 'stone wall of partition' to the Court of Israel. This 'wall of partition' was, Paul told the Ephesians, the dividing wall which — metaphorically speaking — he was concerned to demolish. In Christ, said Paul, there was no Jew nor Gentile, bond nor free, rich nor poor, male nor female, black nor white: just Christian (see Ephesians 2:14).

At that stage the intervention of soldiers from the Roman garrison at the Antonia Fortress saved Paul from being lynched. However, regardless of the rights and wrongs of the situation, the Roman governor would have been jittery when he heard 'that the whole city of Jerusalem was in uproar'. Hence Paul's arrest. But even after his arrest it was necessary for the garrison commander to order that Paul be '*carried* to the barracks' at the Antonia Fortress by the soldiers to prevent a murderous multitude from dismembering him.

While this response is consistent with the Jewish response to Paul throughout his missionary journeys, we, in common with the Roman authorities, are taken aback by the violence that Paul's presence provoked in Jerusalem. The Christians of Caesarea had anticipated correctly. Saul of Tarsus, the turncoat who had set the world on fire with the Christian Gospel, was back where he was known and remembered — and bitterly resented.

Paul was on the steps of the Antonia Fortress. Behind him was the Arch of Ecce Homo. Below him was the Lithostratos or courtyard. Paul knew full well that, thirty years before, from that same spot, Another had faced a murderous multitude. Then they had cried 'Crucify!' Now they cried 'Away with him!' None of that would have been lost on Paul.

The soldiers were understandably eager to hustle Paul into the barracks. But with a strong sense of occasion, Paul succeeded in controlling the situation sufficiently to ask the commander for permission to speak. Amazed that Paul could speak Greek, and under the impression that he was an Egyptian terrorist, the commander was understandably reluctant. Paul was urgent: 'I am a Jew, from Tarsus in Cilicia, a citizen of no mean city. Please let me speak to the people.'

There must have been a presence about Paul. Permission granted, he proceeded to still the murderous multitude. He spoke to them in Aramaic; 'they became very quiet'. He reminded them who he was, about his education in the city under Gamaliel, of his zeal for God, how he had thrown Christians into prison 'as also the high priest and all the Council can testify'. Then, Paul amazes us: he told them of his complicity in the murder of Stephen, of his journey to Damascus, of his meeting with the risen Christ, of his baptism, and of the Lord's commission that he take the Gospel to the Gentiles. The crowd's response? '"Rid the earth of him! He's not fit to live!"' (Acts 22:22.)

Pandemonium again. The Roman commander, though relieved that Paul was no terrorist, like another Roman facing another multitude with another Prisoner, ordered that Paul be flogged. But Paul turned on the commander and asked crisply; 'Is it legal for you to flog a Roman citizen who hasn't been found guilty?' Taken aback, the commander admitted that he had had to buy his own citizenship. Paul responded: '*But I was born a citizen.*'

The commander's mind was totally confused by the accusations brought against Paul by the Jews, and completely bewildered at the strength of feeling against him. He ordered the Sanhedrin to assemble and released Paul so that he could appear before it. That was like putting Daniel on trial before the lions! High priest Ananias was soon ordering 'those standing near Paul to strike him on the mouth'. But the emotive circumstances had not clouded Paul's judgement. His riposte: 'God will strike you, you whitewashed wall! You sit there to judge me according to the law, yet you yourself violate the law by commanding that I be struck!'

Perhaps it was then that Paul remembered that Jesus had made a different response when He had been slapped. Whatever the reason, Paul apologized to the high priest.

A heated altercation ensued between the Pharisees and the Sadducees on the Sanhedrin. For the second time the Roman commander began to fear that Paul was about to be lynched — and removed him to the barracks. There, overnight, as in Corinth, the risen Lord stood before Paul: 'Take courage! As you have testified about me in Jerusalem, so you must also testify in Rome.'

Meanwhile, in the hours of darkness, the Jews were conspiring to accomplish by stealth what the crowd had failed to accomplish in anger: the murder of Paul. A plot was hatched involving forty men. The 'chief priest and elders' were informed of the plot and, apparently, agreed to co-operate in creating the circumstances for a murder. But the conspiracy was not watertight; Paul's nephew heard of it and entered the barracks at the Antonia to tell him of it. Paul told his nephew to tell the Roman commander what he knew.

That night at nine, it was back to Caesarea for Paul. To ensure his safety the commander ordered that he be accompanied by two hundred soldiers, seventy horsemen and two hundred spearmen. Paul himself was provided with a horse.

The Roman commander in Jerusalem had decided that this matter was sufficiently serious as to be dealt with by Felix the governor. And Felix, according to Cornelius Tacitus in his *Histories*, 'exercised the power of a king with the mind of a slave . . . '.

Readings
Acts 18:18-23.
Acts 19:21-22.
Acts 20:1-6, 13-37.
Acts 21:17-36.
Acts 22:22-23:23.

15

CAESAREA, CRETE – AND
STORMS AT SEA

A letter informed Felix of the circumstances surrounding
Paul's arrest. The governor digested its contents and ordered
that the prisoner 'be kept under guard in Herod's Palace'.
The Sanhedrin was told to prepare the case for the prosecution.

This Antonius Felix was, in many ways, the shape of the
future for the Roman Empire. He was procurator of Judea
from AD52 to 59. The Emperor Claudius appointed him
because he was the brother of Pallas, his favourite at court.
And it would appear that the two brothers had much in common. In Rome, Pallas, while telling Claudius everything he
wanted to hear, was also paying court to his wife and her
son to a previous marriage, Nero. Hence, when Nero succeeded in 54, Pallas became chief adviser. Felix was governed
by ambition and was not the sort of man to be squeamish
about butchering Jews, nor being too sensitive as to the rights
of an individual Jew – albeit a Roman citizen – when it
came to establishing his reputation as a strong man likely to
climb the ladder in Nero's empire.

When the trial was convened five days after Paul's arrival,
the shrewd Roman lawyer, Tertullus, hired by the high priest
Ananias, knew Felix well enough to appeal to his vanity and
ambition in a windy preliminary to his speech. Part of the
charge was that Paul was 'a ring-leader of the Nazarene sect'.
Prosecution strategy against Paul resembled that against
Jesus; his offences were against the Jews, the temple – 'and
Caesar'. Paul's response was that he was a loyal citizen of
Rome and a loyal son of Israel. He made no bones about
being 'a follower of the Way, which they call a sect'.

Tertullus underestimated his opponent; Paul was by no
means an innocent abroad. He homed in on what he considered to be the nub of the issue; a charge brought by absent
Jews from Asia and the Sadducee objection to his preaching
of the resurrection.

At that point Felix adjourned the proceedings. Through

his Jewish wife, Drusilla, he 'was well acquainted with the Way'. He was also doubtless aware of Gallio's decision at the *bema* in Corinth; the Jews had no case under Roman law and he should acquit. But the main consideration on the mind of Felix was not the verdict, but the effect of the verdict upon the populace, and the way that effect might influence his upward mobility. As is often the case, along with ambition Felix harboured avarice; 'He was hoping that Paul would offer him a bribe, so he sent for him frequently and talked with him.' (Acts 24:26.)

The adjournment lasted two years. The trial had initially convened in the early months of AD58. But Nero's Rome, a long way from Caesarea geographically, crept close politically during that period. So close, in fact, that Felix dared not reach a decision one way or another.

For Felix, ambition acted like paralysis. In the spring of 59 Caesarea erupted in riot and Felix was recalled to Rome in disgrace. Only the influence of Pallas prevented his execution. He never held public office again.

Meanwhile, Paul continued in custody.

The new procurator of Judea was Porcius Festus. Exactly how important Paul's case was, and the fact that it might have been an element in the riot that removed Felix from office, is indicated by the fact that three days after his arrival Festus went to Jerusalem to discuss Paul's case with the Jewish establishment. He was under pressure from the high priest to move Paul to Jerusalem (where the conspiracy to murder him would have chance of success). But Festus insisted that the trial continue in Caesarea.

After eight or ten days Festus went down to Caesarea. The very next day he reconvened the trial of Paul. The prosecution's case had not changed, nor had Paul's defence; 'I have done nothing wrong against the law of the Jews or against the temple or against Caesar.'

Perhaps Festus, like Felix before him, was looking beyond the verdict to its probable effect. An acquittal was out of the question, so what was to be done? In open court he asked Paul whether he would be prepared to stand trial in Jerusalem.

Cornered, Paul pursued the only legal course open to him, and exerted the right of every Roman citizen: 'I am now standing before Caesar's court, where I ought to be tried. I have not done any wrong to the Jews, as you yourself know very well. If, however, I am guilty of doing anything deserving death, I do not refuse to die. But if the charges brought against me by these Jews are not true, no one has the right to hand me over to them. *I appeal to Caesar!*'

There was a conference between Festus and his advisers. Then he employed the time-honoured formula: 'You've appealed to Caesar. To Caesar you will go!'

Paul had had two years to plan his strategy. The risen Christ had told him he must go to Rome. Gallio's ruling might even have given him some confidence in Roman justice, though the rumours coming from Nero's Rome must have reached Paul's ears.

Meanwhile, Festus was not completely free of the problem posed by Paul. Not understanding the charges against Paul, he had wrong-footed himself. The first prisoner of his governorship had been referred to Rome. Yet, under Roman law, there were no charges against him and no case to answer. That, Festus knew, would be crystal clear to Nero. Festus was obviously aware of the fate of his predecessor. He was also aware that the terrorist movement, the *sicarii*, that had arisen under his predecessor, was reaching new heights of audacity. The way out suggested itself when client-King Herod Agrippa II arrived in Caesarea on a state visit. His grasp of Jewish politics and religion, surely, would enable him to advise on a form of indictment.

Hence, in an audience room of Herod's Palace, with the Roman establishment at Caesarea looking on, Paul appeared before 32-year-old Agrippa. Agrippa's father, Herod Agrippa I, who had sought to execute the apostle Peter, had died at Tyre in horrendous fashion detailed by the Roman historians and in the book of Acts. Herod Agrippa II was the brother of Drusilla, wife of the disgraced Felix, and of Bernice. Bernice was with him as 'with great pomp' he entered the audience room where Paul was waiting. Emperors Caligula and Nero both had incestuous relationships; contemporary reports would have us believe that that was the nature of Agrippa's relationship with Bernice. But Paul addressed Agrippa with courtesy, acknowledging his expertise in Jewish affairs.

While Agrippa had expressed his eagerness to hear Paul, there can be no doubt that he got a great deal more than he bargained for. In his lengthy speech, Paul did not confine himself to a defence against the specific points upon which he was accused as he had done before Felix and Festus. What Agrippa and Bernice heard was his complete spiritual testimony. Here was an unexpected forum in which Paul could preach Christ.

Paul's trial before Felix had come to an abrupt end at his mention of the resurrection. As he did so before Agrippa, the client-king's grasp of Jewish theology would have enabled him to understand Paul's assertions. But Festus had no such background. He interrupted Paul with the words: 'You are out of your mind, Paul! . . . Your great learning is driving you insane.'

Perhaps Paul continued with a smile. It was, maybe, also with a smile that Agrippa responded to Paul when he had finished with the words: 'Do you think that in such a short time you can persuade me to be a Christian?'

No one can doubt the sincerity of Paul's response: 'Short time or long — I pray God that not only you but all who are listening to me today may become what I am, except for these chains.'

At that Agrippa, Bernice and Festus left. Luke overheard Agrippa say to the procurator: 'This man could have been set free if he had not appealed to Caesar.' No matter what his sins of the flesh might have been, Agrippa gave it as his opinion that Paul had done nothing to deserve imprisonment, let alone death.

Of the three who sat in judgement on Paul, Porcius Festus, his health broken, died within the year. Agrippa ruled Judea for a further seven years until the beginning of the Jewish rebellion in AD66. In that year, with Bernice, he fled to Rome. In Rome, later, Bernice would become mistress to the Emperor Titus who, in AD70, destroyed Jerusalem and slaughtered its inhabitants.

Paul's journey to Rome began in late August AD60. A centurion, Julius, who belonged to the Imperial Regiment and travelled through the empire on escort duties, arrived in Caesarea to escort the prisoners to Rome. Of the group of prisoners, Paul was the only man of rank. He was permitted two assistants: Luke, the physician, and Aristarcus of Thessalonica.

Though in chains, Paul was allowed a degree of freedom. When they put in at Sidon, sixty-nine nautical miles north, Paul was permitted to meet friends who had brought provisions for him. He might even have gone for a meal with them while the ship was being unloaded and reloaded. It was customary for passengers to go ashore while that was in progress.

When Paul had sailed into Tyre more than two years previously, the route had been to the west of the island of Cyprus. In reverse direction, the same route was taken. Prevailing winds in late August and September were westerly or north-westerly. Hence the vessel making for Myra near Attalia in Asia Minor would have made for the open sea.

Luke's account of that sea journey is amazing for its precision and vividness. This is a clear indication that Luke was of the party.

At Myra, Julius, the centurion, arranged for a change of vessels. They went aboard an Alexandrian grain ship bound for Italy. The fact that a ship from Alexandria bound for Italy should have been found in the harbour at Myra is to be accounted for by the fact that ancient ships were not well designed for sailing against the wind. Hence it was natural for ships from Alexandria to sail more or less due north — putting in at Myra. Thereafter the navigator would have sought to take advantage of the coast of Asia Minor for the next stage of the journey. The intention would have been to arrive in Italy before the onset of winter.

The weather deteriorated sooner than expected. The ship proceeded westwards but only with great difficulty. It reached

Cnidus, a peninsula forming the south-west tip of Asia Minor. The north-westerly wind was proving too strong.

After Cnidus, the natural route would have been towards **Crete** and along the north side of the island. However, on that occasion, the ship rounded the east tip of Crete — Cape Salmone — in order to continue west on the south or lee side of the island.

It was becoming clear that they would not complete their voyage to Italy before winter. Hence, when they put in at Fair Havens, it is likely that they were planning to sit out the weather. Bad weather must have necessitated the choice of Fair Havens, a wide, open bay, because under normal circumstances no good captain would have chosen such a poor harbour.

The voyage from Caesarea had already taken a considerable length of time. As a result, the date had arrived on which seafaring normally came to a standstill for the winter. The Day of Atonement was already past and, in AD60, it had fallen on 5 October. Roman military writer Vegetius states that navigation was considered dangerous after 15 September and that it ceased for the winter from 11 November.

Paul was almost certainly the most seasoned traveller aboard. Despite his prisoner status, therefore, he had the authority to say: 'Men, I can see that our voyage is going to be disastrous and bring great loss to ship and cargo, and to our own lives also.'

But the advice of the owner of the ship was contrary to that of Paul. He had a cargo to deliver before winter. Since, in any event, Fair Havens was unsuitable for overwintering, the centurion took the owner's advice and the vessel put to sea.

Assisted by a gentle south wind, the ship hugged the Cretan coast. The objective was to reach Phoenix, only forty miles distant.

But 'a wind of hurricane force' began to blow, perhaps reminiscent of the one we experienced at Mileta in February. But this one was a 'north-easter' that swept down from the Cretan mountains, forcing the ship to 'scud before it'.

As with Rhodes, Crete has many legends associated with

Paul. Cretan tradition identifies Fair Havens with Lasea and its beautiful broad bay. It identifies Phoenix with the bay of Loutro, the tiny town clustered on the seashore at the foot of precipitous cliffs. The assumption is made that Paul and his party put ashore. Fragments of marble have been found on two Pauline sites, together with the foundations of early-date churches. A white chapel built on the brow of a hill overlooking the Fair Havens bay commemorates Paul's arrival on the island. This was built on the site of a much earlier church. A few yards to the west of it is the traditional cave and chapel of St. Paul, the cave marked by a tall cross. The Cretans insist that Paul preached at Hierapetra.

The people of Loutro (Phoenix) maintain that Paul visited their town either on that or on a later journey. They have an ancient church and a spring named after him. The church can only be reached by boat. Cretans believe that Paul baptized his first Cretan converts here.

Visitors to Heracleon on Crete will be shown the cathedral of St. Titus, will hear the claim that the epistle to Titus provides evidence that Paul had a wide knowledge and experience of the island and, further, that he had evangelized it after being released from his first imprisonment in Rome. This is referred to as Paul's 'fourth missionary journey'. At Gortyna, the island's capital, it is asserted that Paul consecrated Titus bishop of the island.

For once the facts of the case back up the tradition. In his letter to Titus, Paul writes, 'I left you in Crete . . . that you might straighten out what was left unfinished and appoint elders in every town, as I directed you. . . .' (1:5.) When Paul goes on to warn Titus of the 'talkers and deceivers' of the Law Party (verse 10) who were 'ruining whole households by teaching things they ought not to teach — and that for the sake of dishonest gain' (verse 11), he continues: 'Even one of their own prophets has said, "Cretans are always liars, evil brutes, lazy gluttons." ' (verse 12.) Paul continues, 'this testimony is true' and counsels Titus to 'rebuke them sharply' (verse 13) and even goes so far as to say 'they must be silenced' (verse 11). In his commentary on Titus, William Barclay considers it a real probability that, in between his first and second imprisonments in Rome, Paul undertook evangelistic work in various localities, including Crete and — drawing his inference from Romans 15:24 and 28 — Spain.

Crete certainly had an importance in the ancient world which it does not have today. Homer had referred to 'Crete of the hundred cities'. From his days in Tarsus, Paul would have known of the importance and riches of populous Crete. Wherever he went he must have considered the 'gospel-potential' of an area. And when the ship was at anchor in the bay of Fair Havens, he must have thought of the imperative of bringing Christ to the Cretans . . . .

The Cretans are ready to admit that Paul's negative quotation about their forefathers in Titus 1:12 rings true. 'The ancient world spoke of the three most evil Cs — the Cretans, Cilicians, and the Cappadocians.' 'In the ancient world', they told us, 'the Cretans were famed as a drunken, insolent, untrustworthy, lying, and gluttonous people . . . '. Against that, the modern Cretan Christians set the fact that to them, as to their ancestors, Paul preached 'the grace of God that brings salvation . . . to all men' and 'the blessed hope — the glorious appearing of our great God and Saviour, Jesus Christ' (Titus 2:11, 13).

But we have left Paul and his companions in a flimsy vessel at the mercy of a fierce storm that blew down from Crete's Mount Ida.

From the Cretan coast came the stentorian boom of the surf on the beaches. As frantic seamen struggled with the sails, the wind whirled and twisted; the rain drenched and the sky was black. The mainmast shuddered. And that shudder vibrated every timber.

High seas were running. Each wave was higher than the vessel. Immense clouds of spray were flung high into the air like the explosion of giant puffballs, only to fall back in hissing spume upon the crown of the next wave.

Seamen, soldiers and prisoners feared for their lives. But Paul knew he had an appointment in Rome.

———

Readings
> Acts 24:1-22.
> Acts 25:1-12.
> Acts 27:1-15.

16

THE MALTA EXPERIENCE

But before Rome, Paul was to pay an unexpected visit to Malta.

The day we flew into Malta we noted in the Maltese *Times* that Paul was still news on the island. The back page featured the latest research and archaeological findings on Paul's shipwreck. A century ago the Maltese built a monolith of the apostle on an islet off the western fringe of the broad, sandy bay known as St. Paul's Bay.

The islet, apparently, does not accord with the detail provided by Luke in Acts (27:27-29, 39-41; 28:7). The evidence, the scholars argued, points to the rocky headland on the *eastern* fringe of St. Paul's Bay. The headland, in fact, between St. Paul's Bay and Salina Bay. There the sea depths were right and, most importantly, that headland would have been within sight of the House of 'Publius, the chief official of the island' (28:7). That would have been located at or near the city-set-on-a-hill that was the Roman capital of Malta, Melita. Today the hill on which Roman Melita was built accommodates two towns divided by a man-made valley. Hence Roman remains are to be found under both Mdina, called by the Maltese 'the silent city', and Rabat. The artificial valley was created by Aglabid Arabs in 870 to render the Roman citadel — on the part of the high ground that now accommodates Mdina — defensible.

Influenced by these findings, we part climbed and part waded out to the rocky headland. On an early September day with temperatures in the 80s, the sea still smashed with some force against the wall of rock at the extremity of the headland.

Our imaginations pin-wheeled back to November AD60 and the 276 men aboard an Alexandrian grain vessel being driven helplessly before a gale . . . .

Grain vessels of the period were usually large, typically 140 feet long, 36 feet wide, with a draught of 33 feet. But, with their one great square sail, they were hard to manage. On those ancient ships there was neither sextant nor compass; so in cloudy or dark weather there was no means of navigation. The great terror of first-century seamen was the Syrtis sands, the graveyard of ships in the ancient world. Hence, 'they lowered the sea anchor and let the ship be driven along. . . . ' (Act 27:17.)

The 'wind of hurricane force' (verse 14) drove the vessel before it for fourteen days and nights, during which time neither sun nor stars were visible. The captain lost all sense of orientation. The 'violent battering' of the ship on the second day caused him to order that the cargo be thrown overboard. On the third day all extraneous ship's tackle was dumped in the sea.

The anxiety of the 276 complement was such that no one ate. Captain and crew were in fear for their lives. Only Paul remained beyond the grip of the prevailing terror. He sought to infuse courage into all who would listen.

Meanwhile, the pounding breakers shook the timbers of the wooden vessel until it seemed in danger of breaking up. The decision was made that the ship be 'frapped'; hawsers were passed underneath it and the loose timbers of the vessel were tied up like a parcel.

At some point in the storm a curious thing happened. It is likely to have taken place gradually. As passengers and crew lost hope and gave in to terror, one man emerged cool, calm and clear-sighted: Paul. *It is evident that Paul took command of the vessel.* The prisoner became the captain. Paul was, after all, a seasoned seafarer. Before setting out for Rome, the apostle had already made eleven voyages on the Mediterranean. From Ernst Haenchen's *The Acts of the Apostles: A Commentary* (1971), pages 702-703, it is possible to calculate that Paul had travelled at least 3,500 miles by sea.

In addition to Paul's experience with the elements, however, was his intimate knowledge and close relationship with the God who controlled the elements. Even the most experienced and knowledgeable of men can crack in a crisis. That Paul stood straight and firm as mighty seas buffeted the vessel and threatened to thrash it to matchwood is to be accounted for by his knowledge of God and His purposes. Paul heard the voice of reassurance; ''''Do not be afraid.

. . . You must stand trial before Caesar; and God has graciously given you the lives of all who sail with you.' ' ' ' (Acts 27:24.)

On the fourteenth night of the gale, while being driven broadside, the sailors heard the noise of sea thrashing land. Soundings were taken; at first the sea was found to be 120 feet deep, then, at the second sounding only 90 feet deep. Fearing that that was the point at which all would perish, the sailors acted like desperate men. They entered into a conspiracy. They loosed the lifeboat with the intention of leaving passengers behind and taking their own chances of survival. But Paul was ahead of their schemes. He told the centurion that all must remain with the ship if all were to be saved. The centurion gave orders for the ropes that held the lifeboat to be cut. It fell away.

There Paul the theologian, the man of visions, of arguments and of words emerges supremely as the man of action. He insisted that all took some sustenance. They had not eaten for fourteen days. Hungry men were not competent men. Before they ate, he gave the blessing. After they had eaten, the last of the grain was thrown into the sea.

'When daylight came', writes Luke, 'they did not recognize the land, but they saw a bay with a sandy beach, where they decided to run the ship aground if they could. Cutting loose the anchors, they left them in the sea and at the same time untied the ropes that held the rudders. Then they hoisted the foresail to the wind and made for the beach. . . . ' (Acts 27:39, 40.) But, in their efforts to beach the ship, they wrecked it. The bow stuck fast 'and the stern was broken to pieces by the pounding of the surf' (verse 41). The soldiers wanted to kill the prisoners but, in deference to Paul, the centurion ordered them to sheath their swords. The entire 276 complement of the vessel jumped ship. All successfully swam ashore. And the shore was the sandy beach of Malta.

Our visit to Malta was organized by Inter-Church and in company with a party of twenty-five led by Canon Rex Howe. This prosperous, magical island set in a deep blue sea was a source of inspiration to all of us. Our hotel overlooked the Grand Harbour and, through a forest of masts and across an expanse of deep blue water, we could see St. Paul's Anglican cathedral with its steeple, and, beside it, the RC Church of Mount Carmel with its magnificent dome.

Like most in Malta, our guide spoke perfect English. Simone began by establishing the historicity of the Pauline tradition on Malta. The archaeological excavations carried out at San Pawl Milqghi proved 'beyond doubt that Paul's arrival in Malta is a historical fact, and it is also a fact that during his three-month stay on the island he sowed the first seeds of the Christian religion to which Maltese people overwhelmingly belong'.

Under skies only a little paler blue than the sea, we bussed round the sites of the island. Malta is approximately the same size as the Isle of Wight, but its population is many times larger. The roads are very crowded. Theoretically, driving is on the left, but the driving style of the native Maltese is of the adventurous type. Malta has an excellent bus service, despite the fact that the vehicles in use were, in the main, manufactured in Britain in the 1940s and early 1950s. A disproportionate number of cars on the road were of British 1950s vintage, the most common being the split-windscreen Morris Minor. But part of the charm of all of this was that the great majority of these 'vintage' vehicles were bright, shiny, and good as new!

Once she had established as fact Paul's three-month visit to Malta in AD60-61, Simone proceeded to introduce us to the remainder of the island's rich heritage. She left us to find our own way to the Pauline sites on our free days!

Prehistoric sites on Malta are, it must be said, of particular interest. Malta's megalithic temple at Hagar Qim and Gozo's Tarxien temple predate the pyramids.

The Maltese capital, Valletta, was built by La Valette, Grand Master of the Order of St. John, on the steep-sided Mount Sciverras to guard the Grand Harbour against Turkish invasion. One of the two great episodes in their history of which the Maltese are justly proud is their success against the Ottoman Turks in the Great Siege of 1565.

The island of Malta was ruled by the Knights of St. John from the time of Charles V to the time of Napoleon. We visited the 'Co-Cathedral' of St. John in Valletta, as well as the Palace of the Grand Masters of the Knights of St. John nearby. Simone gained access to parts of this palace not normally open and we were able to visit areas occupied by the royal family during the period of British rule. Of course, the second historic episode of which the Maltese are particularly proud is how the island stood out against the ceaseless bombardment by Hitler's Luftwaffe between 1940 and 1943 and, in consequence, how the island was awarded the George Cross.

Malta is an island of churches, and a disproportionate number of these are, not surprisingly, dedicated to St. Paul. In Valletta is the Church of St. Paul Shipwreck. In the 'silent city' of Mdina the Cathedral is dedicated to St. Paul, as is the main church in the other hill-town built over the remains of Roman Melita, Rabat.

Mdina is built as a citadel and from the citadel walls the headland of Paul's shipwreck is clearly visible. Beneath St. Paul's Church, Rabat, are pre-Christian caves. In one of these caves, which contains a marble statue of Paul, it is claimed that he lived during his three-month stay. The other was once part of a Roman prison; however, there is also evidence that it was used for Christian worship and that baptisms by immersion took place there. Perhaps Paul conducted worship services, baptizing his first converts in this place.

Nearby, but accessible through a separate entrance, are the authentic Catacombs of St. Catalous. The central area, it was claimed, was used by early Christians for the agape feasts that they celebrated prior to burials.

The orientation of Malta is towards the sea. No one who visits the three Maltese islands of Malta, Gozo and Comino will be able to resist the temptation to spend time on the blue-to-turquoise waters, visiting the Blue Grotto and blue lagoons.

Paul did not have the best of Malta. He wintered there. During his stay he introduced Publius, the senior Roman official on the island, to Christ, along with many others. He also laid his hands on the father of Publius and healed him of a fever and of dysentery. Thereafter, it would appear that others on the island with ailments came to Paul and Luke for medical attention and healing. That aspect of Paul's ministry is commemorated in the impressive domed church at Mosta. This church is one of the most striking on the island, having been inspired by the Pantheon in Rome. During the Luftwaffe bombardment, a bomb pierced the dome and came to rest amid the vast congregation — but failed to explode!

Our abiding impressions of Malta, Gozo and Comino include the distinctive Phoenician-style boats, baroque churches, the native Maltese who have lost none of the 'unusual kindness' (Acts 28:2) that Paul encountered and those moments of meditation on the headland. Here, or somewhere near here, in November AD60, 276 men came ashore from a shipwreck, all of whom owed their lives to a prisoner who had taken command in a crisis.

But Paul's prisoner-status did not change on Malta. And with the first sign of better weather he was on board another ship. The destination was the same. Rome.

Readings
Acts 27:13-28:10.

17

PAUL IN ROME

The centurion and contingent of the Imperial Regiment who had accompanied Paul from Caesarea had, doubtless, been kicking their heels all winter. They were eager to be in Rome and be free of their charge.

An Alexandrian grain ship, like the one shipwrecked the previous November, had been wintering in Malta. On its prow were figureheads of the twin gods Castor and Pollux. The centurion booked a passage for his party aboard the ship which, we may infer, sailed with the first spell of good weather in AD61.

The voyage to Syracuse in Sicily was uneventful, as was the onward journey to Rhegium on the toe of Italy. From there, still on board ship, they journeyed up to Puteoli, the port of Rome.

As he disembarked, Paul would have been less than human had he not felt similar tremors to those he had experienced when entering Corinth years before. After all, Rome ruled the world; its legions were everywhere; nowhere where he had travelled could its edicts have been ignored.

Puteoli was where the grain ships put in; it had many wharfs and warehouses and a cosmopolitan population.

From the wharfs of Puteoli, Paul might have looked north and seen the mighty Roman fleets at anchor off Misenum; and reflected on the power of Rome.

If he looked south he would have seen the broad beaches of Baiae, the playground of wealthy Romans; and he would have thought of the corruption that was Rome.

Though flanked by Luke and Aristarcus, Paul might have felt timid and alone as he set off on the Appian Way that connected the coast with Rome.

Forty-three miles south-west of Rome was the Forum of Appius. Nearby were the Three Taverns. There, to Paul's immense relief and joy, a significant party of Roman Christians had come out to greet him. The Greek word used to cover Paul's meeting with the deputation is one normally used for a city deputation going out to greet a conquering hero. It is likely that, to them, Paul was just that. Since Jesus,

Christianity had produced no greater hero than Paul, apostle to the Gentiles.

Paul took courage from his encounter. A theme that runs through his letters is his dependence upon friends. Paul was the bravest of the brave, and a great leader of men. Nevertheless, his leadership was of a sort that a captain exerts over his team. Wherever he went, Paul made friends and when he came to write his letters to the churches he painstakingly greeted his friends by name, carefully recalling their qualities and their contribution. Again and again Paul recorded his debt to those like Luke, Timothy, Silas, Barnabas, John Mark and Tychicus, who were his 'fellow-labourers' and 'whose names were written in the book of life'. Nor was Paul slow to acknowledge the invaluable help he had received from 'those women which laboured with me in the Gospel'. (Philippians 4:3, KJV.)

On a typical anti-cyclonic March morning, under cloudless skies and bright sunshine, we followed Paul's route along the Appian Way towards Rome. We had begun the morning being conducted by a priest around the Catacombs of St. Calixtus; and, in their dark, labyrinthine ways, had heard echoes of a Church beyond Paul's time, under persecution, in hiding among the dead but celebrating the living Christ.

Back in Rome we had a curious wish to find some high spot from which to overview the city. We had already pored over the arches and ruins of ancient Rome. But we had yet to derive a picture in our imaginations of the Rome to which the apostles came. Sitting among the students and spring flowers on the Spanish Steps, we asked advice. There was only one place that afforded an overview of the city, we were told, and it was the topmost cupola above the dome of St. Peter's!

Soon we were pacing the Via della Conciliazione towards the Basilica of St. Peter. On earlier occasions we had marvelled at the magnificent piazza of Bernini with its fountains and porticoes. The obelisk at the centre of the piazza was much photographed; it had, we knew, come from Heliopolis and been brought to Rome by Caligula and placed at the centre of Nero's circus where, ironically, the Vatican now stands . . . .

All Protestant propensities notwithstanding, like millions before us we had admired Michelangelo's great basilica. We had even pursued the warren of corridors beneath it and examined 'The Tomb of St. Peter' as well as the tombs of many of the popes. But to climb to the top of the topmost cupola . . . .

The noon heat found us climbing to the gallery around the inner curve of the dome of St. Peter's; the package pilgrims looked like ants below. Then there was a further exhausting climb to the topmost cupola of the dome — ringed around by an external walkway — and our reward of the unparalleled view of the Piazza of St. Peter, the Vatican gardens and the great city beyond.

Below us, looking out over the Piazza, was the great stone figure of Christ and, in parallel, the figures of all the disciples.

But where was Paul?

We looked over this great city built on seven hills. We glanced south towards the entry of the Appian Way to the gateway through which the 61-year-old Jewish scholar, chained to two members of the Imperial Regiment, entered the city, surrounded by an enthusiastic crowd of Christians.

As the palaces, theatres, amphitheatres, temples and great buildings of Rome burst upon the eye of Paul, he knew that he was entering the greatest city on earth. Perhaps someone pointed out Nero's palace on the Palatine, and then the large ornamental lake that Nero was having excavated for his pleasure (where the Colosseum now stands). Paul would have walked the streets of old Rome, and seen the forums. But, beyond them, he would have glimpsed the ramshackle that housed the hundreds of thousands of poor.

But it was not among the poor that Paul was lodged. The two years he spent in Rome before his first trial would have been in a sizeable house for which he paid the rent. Almost certainly the house would have been within the walls of the city near the camp of the Praetorian Guard on the Caelian Hill, in the north quarter of the city. From our vantage point atop St. Peter's we could identify the approximate area.

Paul had lodged in a noisy part of the city. As well as the

military din of arriving and departing legions, parades and reviews, there was the jostle of the market places and, from time to time, the distant roar of the Circus Maximus where chariot races and gladiatorial combats took place.

But Paul, apparently, did not give himself time to be overawed by Rome. Consistent with his practice in every city he had visited previously, he made contact with the Jewish leaders. As objectively as he could, he outlined his situation to them. Only the conclusion of his speech was emotive; 'It is because of the hope of Israel that I am bound with this chain.' (Acts 28:20.)

The reply of the Jewish leaders was a studied one. Rome was not Caesarea. Nor was Nero Felix. In Palestine the Sanhedrin carried clout, because behind its declarations was the menace of popular rising. In Rome Jewish opinion had never been significant and since the decree of Claudius had scarcely existed.

Hence the response of the Jewish leaders to Paul's speech was a muted one. It is most unlikely that word had not spread from Jerusalem or Caesarea about Paul, given the length of time since his initial arrest. Nevertheless, they denied having had news of Paul from Judea, either favourable or unfavourable; '"But we want to hear what your views are, for we know that people everywhere are talking against this sect."' (Verse 22.) Perhaps the last clause was the most significant.

Paul never missed an opportunity to preach Christ, nor did he do so then. Commensurate with his normal practice, he expounded the messianic passages of the Old Testament and identified Jesus in them. 'Some were convinced by what he said, but others would not believe.' (Verse 24.) They began to argue among themselves. Doubtless with sadness in his voice, Paul used a quotation from Isaiah which implied a Jewish rejection of Jesus. He had, after all, been offering them the message of the Gospel for thirty years and, while a few had always accepted, most had slammed the door shut and then, behind it, begun to conspire. In Rome, as elsewhere, Paul took the slamming of the door by the Jews to be the opening of the door of opportunity for the Gentiles.

From his place of house arrest Paul welcomed all who

came to see him (verse 30). And so Luke concluded the book of Acts with the picture of Paul's preaching the Gospel in Rome 'without let or hindrance'. For Luke that was a triumphant picture. But for us, as the conclusion to a book, it leaves many questions unanswered.

Thankfully, the biography of Paul is not contained only in Acts but is interspersed all over the place, in Paul's letters to both churches and individuals. And thus we can piece a picture together.

The two years during which Paul waited to be tried before Nero were filled with activity. In addition to preaching in his home, he was obliged to earn his living. Indeed, to meet expenses, including his rent, Paul might well have had to ply his tentmaking trade more strenuously than at most other periods in his life.

Over and above that there was the task of preparing teachers and evangelists for the populous cities of Italy and beyond. Evidence suggests that the Roman church itself was fairly numerous and, in the absence of any firm evidence that Peter was present at that stage, it is likely that Paul carried the main pastoral responsibility. He remembered with gratitude the labour he had expended two years earlier on the most complete testament of faith he had ever written: the Letter to the Romans. Still rewarding study nineteen-and-a-half centuries later, it had, we can be sure, proved a tremendous blessing to Roman Christians of Paul's day.

But Paul's pastoral responsibility was not restricted to Rome. His letters suggest that he never forgot a single soul in a single church in any country. The letters further suggest that, far from being cut off there in his prison, Paul was in touch with all of the latest currents of thought. In his letter to the church at Colossae he showed an awareness, surprising for his time, of the menace of Gnosticism. And then, as he wrote to the churches at Ephesus, Philippi, as well as Colossae, there were the older enemies: the occult, astrology, and the ever-infuriating activities of the Law Party.

But there is joy in Paul's prison letters. Indeed, joy is the main theme of his letter to the Philippians. From that letter we derive a picture of a prisoner in Rome who, far from bemoaning his lot, is, as in the Philippian gaol, singing hymns at midnight.

Paul would begin each day with prayer. The guard to whom he was chained would have been obliged to accompany Paul upon his knees, and to listen to his outpouring of words of thankfulness, intercession, and hope. Perhaps it was a pagan Roman soldier who was the first to hear Paul utter in prayer the soaring words we find in Ephesians 3:20, 21, (KJV): 'Now unto him that is able to do exceeding abundantly above all that we ask or think, according to the power that worketh in us, unto him be glory in the church by Christ Jesus throughout all ages, world without end. Amen.'

We may speculate how long it was possible to remain a pagan in Paul's presence; how many guards left duty with hearts softened by the love of Jesus.

There were days, we may be sure, when that rented house on the Caelian Hill was a hive of activity, comings and goings. By the end of AD61, Timothy and Tychicus were part of Paul's party in Rome. And there was Aristarcus and Luke 'the beloved physician' who had lived with him through the shipwreck and the Malta experience. There was Demas, Epaphras — and there was the runaway slave Onesimus . . . .

In the midst of dictating his letters to the Ephesians, the Colossians and the Philippians, Paul had to deal with the problem of Onesimus. That necessitated the only entirely personal letter contained in the canon of Scripture: Philemon.

Colossae in Asia had long since been evangelized. Philemon was among its foremost Christian leaders. And Onesimus had been his slave. But Onesimus had escaped. Like many escaped slaves he had drifted to Rome. It would have taken him some time. A more obvious place to have lost himself might have been Ephesus. But Ephesus was too near to home. He might be found. And when a runaway slave was recaptured the automatic penalty was death. So Onesimus had come to Rome. And in Rome his life had been transformed by the power of the Gospel of Christ. He had become part of Paul's household.

How would Paul square things with Philemon? A letter was called for.

'Onesimus' meant 'useful', and Paul decided to make the most of a pun; 'I appeal to you for my son Onesimus, who became my son while I was in chains. Formally he was useless to you, but now he has become useful both to you and to me. . . . ' (Philemon 10 and 11).

The letter to Philemon was sent from Paul's rented house in Rome in AD62. Tychicus, often Paul's secretary, was absent. Hence Timothy might have had to write the letter. But Onesimus himself had to take it to his former master (verse 12). Paul invited Philemon to receive him as a brother in Christ. Paul had already told the Ephesians that in Christ Jesus 'there is neither bond nor free'. Paul was in confident mood as he finished his letter to Philemon, inviting him to 'prepare a guest room for me . . . '.

At length the two years of waiting came to an end. Paul had his hearing before Caesar. 'Pray for me,' he had urged the Ephesians, 'that whenever I open my mouth, words may be given me so that I will fearlessly make known the mystery of the gospel, for which I am an ambassador in chains.' (6:19, 20.)

While the earlier Caesars had routinely heard cases referred up to them, Nero had avoided personal jurisdiction in the earlier part of his reign and had delegated capital cases while reserving the right to confirm the sentences afterwards. Hence Praetorian prefects like Burrus or Tigellinus had heard many cases. However, the indications are that the ever-whimsical Nero had, early in AD62 and for his personal amusement, begun to preside over capital cases in a special hall put aside for the purpose in his palace on the Palatine.

Cornelius Tacitus in *The Annals of Imperial Rome* and Gaius Suetonius in *The Twelve Caesars* are unanimous in their negative verdict on Nero and in the historical details they provide of his life. Initially, this thoroughly debauched and incestuous Caesar had married the daughter of his predecessor, Claudius. However, by the time he came to try Paul, he had divorced her to marry Poppaea, previously the wife of a close friend. Poppaea was, if anything, more debauched than Nero himself and is considered to have encouraged him in many of his perverted practices and in his abuse of power. She had also, ironically, dabbled in Judaism; she certainly had contacts in the Jewish community. None of that should have worked in Paul's favour.

Though, at one stage, Paul had had a considerable number of friends in Rome, at the time of his trial he felt very much alone. Tychicus was away in Ephesus. Titus was in Dalmatia. Crescens had been sent to Galatia. There was an urgency in Paul's appeal to Timothy; 'Do your best to come to me quickly, for Demas, because he loved this world, has deserted me and has gone to Thessalonica. . . . Only Luke is with me. . . . At my first defence, no one came to my support, but everyone deserted me. . . . But the Lord stood at my side and gave me strength . . . .' (2 Timothy 4:9-17.)

Nevertheless, concluded Paul, 'I was delivered from the lion's mouth. . . . ' (Verse 17). Perhaps, as John Pollock suggests in *The Apostle* (1969), page 229, 'Whatever their personal reactions to Paul's plain speaking, the distinguished consuls and senators who sat as assessors apparently gave a majority vote in his favour, and Nero — who often ignored the majority opinion — acquitted.'

At all events, the balance of probability is that Paul left the palace on the Palatine a free man.

How long he enjoyed his freedom is the subject of dispute. His eventual execution is likely to have come about at the time of the great fire of Rome only two years later.

Christian writers speculate that in the period between his acquittal and eventual execution, Paul visited Spain, Crete and, possibly, Colossae.

Whether Paul's re-arrest occurred in Asia or in Rome we do not know. However, the background that led to his arrest and execution can be gleaned from the writings of Cornelius Tacitus in his *The Annals of Imperial Rome*. By AD64 Nero's second marriage had ended in divorce. His third, according to Tacitus, was 'a homosexual marriage'. . . . On the day it was contracted, says Tacitus, the fire 'began in the circus, where it adjoins the Palatine and Caelian Hills.' The wind fanned it through shops, the full length of the circus, until it lapped at the walls of the mansions, temples and palaces on the Palatine. After that, 'the ancient city's narrow, winding streets and irregular blocks encouraged its progress.'

No attempt was made, apparently, to fight the flames. By contrast, Tacitus asserted, men were seen throwing torches and fanning the flames. Tantalizingly, he added; 'Perhaps they had received orders . . . .'

The fire lasted for six days. At the end of it, 'of Rome's fourteen districts, only four remained intact. Three were levelled to the ground.'

The rumour spread that somehow Nero himself had been responsible for the fire. 'To suppress this rumour, Nero fabricated scapegoats — and punished with every refinement the notoriously depraved Christians (as they were popularly called).' Tacitus went on to provide one of the firmest evidences from a secular historian to the historicity of Jesus; 'Their originator, Christ, had been executed in Tiberius' reign by the governor of Judaea, Pontius Pilatus. But in spite of this temporary setback the deadly superstition had broken out afresh, not only in Judaea (where the mischief had started) but even in Rome. All degraded and shameful practices collect and flourish in the capital . . . .'

His undoubted hostility to Christianity notwithstanding, Tacitus stated; 'Despite their guilt as Christians, and the ruthless punishment it deserved, the victims were pitied. For it was felt that they were being sacrificed to one man's brutality rather than to the national interest.'

At first, Tacitus stated, 'Nero had self-acknowledged Christians arrested.' The emperor had chosen the Christians as scapegoats because they were *odio humani generis* ('because the human race detested them'). Tacitus detailed the grisly deaths the Christians died. Some were set alight. Some were torn to pieces by dogs. Others were crucified.

Tradition has it that Paul was beheaded and buried outside the walls of Rome.

On our last day in Rome we went to the Church of St. Paul built over the traditional site of his tomb. In the coolth of this basilica we took time to pray and meditate on Christ's great champion. We thought of the great letter he had written to the Roman Christians and how it has been the catalyst of so many reformations and revivals in Christian history.

From St. Paul's outside the walls of Rome, we trekked to St. John Lateran. The original St. John Lateran was built by Constantine in 313. However, the present structure is seventeenth-century Baroque. Adjoining was the papal palace. Across the road was the Sancta Scala. Pilgrims were toiling up it, kissing each stair.

What had become the official religion of the Roman Empire under Constantine had been a convenient mixture, only one ingredient of which came out of the New Testament.

It had fallen to the lot of Martin Luther to clear away the debris of pious practice and paganism to expose the foundation stone of the Christianity preached by Paul: 'The just shall live by faith.' This was a truth that, after years of study and exposition of the book of Romans, crystallized in Luther's brain as, like the pilgrims in front of us, he had toiled up the Sancta Scala.

The footprints of Paul were stilled in Rome. We could follow him no farther.

What was the state of Paul's mind as he awaited his execution?

We can only conjecture. Unless, that is, with John Pollock, we take the view that Paul's second letter to Timothy was written before his eventual execution, not his first trial.

Whatever view we take, Paul's attitude of mind, consistent for so many years, is likely to have been unaltered.

'I am now ready to be offered, and the time of my departure is at hand. I have fought a good fight, I have finished my course, I have kept the faith: henceforth there is laid up for me a crown of righteousness, which the Lord, the righteous judge, shall give me at that day.' (2 Timothy 4:6-8, KJV.)

The closing scene, then, is Nero's Rome. And an axe is about to fall. But as Paul had once seen the light of eternity shine from the eyes of the dying Stephen, now it shone from his own eyes.

His body was in Rome. But his hope was the blessed hope.

No caesar of a corrupt empire could dispel the shining in his eyes, for it reflected 'the Lord, the righteous Judge' and 'the crown of glory'.

If we follow the footprints of Paul we can go no further than Rome. If we grasp the Gospel he preached we shall enter — with Paul and all who have 'kept the faith' — the everlasting empire of the only righteous King.

Somewhere near the third milestone on the Ostian Way a nameless executioner, at the orders of an infamous emperor, ended the life of Christ's greatest champion. An inscription from Paul's writings, near the spot, still speaks his Gospel: 'Who shall separate us from the love of Christ? Shall tribulation . . . or sword?'

The axe has fallen. But who has triumphed? Death has not separated Paul from the love of Christ. He is assured of the inheritance of the saints. He is no castaway; his will be the high calling in Christ Jesus. For he has been found in Christ, not having his own righteousness, but the righteousness which is of God by faith. The 'thorn in the flesh' can no longer sting; his rebuffs and reversals are over. What better ending? The best is yet to be. When the Lord Himself shall descend from heaven and a numberless multitude shall gather by a sea of glass there will be thousands — from the highlands of Galatia, the seaboard of Asia Minor, the sin centres of Greece, the power centre of Rome, and wherever the footprints of Paul have been — looking for the one who introduced them to Jesus.

Readings
Acts 28:11-30; 2 Timothy 4.